Thomas Cook

TRAVELLERS

ALBANIA

By
**JEROEN VAN MARLE AND
RICHARD SCHOFIELD**

Written by Jeroen van Marle and Richard Schofield
Original photography by Jeroen van Marle and Richard Schofield

Published by Thomas Cook Publishing
A division of Thomas Cook Tour Operations Limited.
Company registration no. 1450464 England
The Thomas Cook Business Park, Unit 9, Coningsby Road,
Peterborough PE3 8SB, United Kingdom
Email: books@thomascook.com, Tel: + 44 (0) 1733 416477
www.thomascookpublishing.com

Produced by Cambridge Publishing Management Limited
Burr Elm Court, Main Street, Caldecote CB23 7NU

ISBN: 978-1-84848-075-9

First edition © 2009 Thomas Cook Publishing
Text © Thomas Cook Publishing
Maps © Thomas Cook Publishing/PCGraphics (UK) Limited

Series Editor: Maisie Fitzpatrick
Production/DTP: Steven Collins

Printed and bound in Italy by Printer Trento

Cover photography: Front L–R: © Matjaz Tancic/Alamy;
© bildagentur-online.com/Alamy; © Donald Nausbaum/Alamy
Back: © Robert Harding/Alamy

The paper used for this book has been independently certified as having
been sourced from well-managed forests and other controlled sources
according to the rules of the Forest Stewardship Council.
This book has been printed and bound in Italy by Printer Trento S.r.l.,
an FSC certified company for printing books on FSC mixed paper in
compliance with the chain of custody and on products labelling standards.

FSC
Mixed Sources
Product group from well-managed
forests and other controlled sources
Cert no. CQ-COC-000012
www.fsc.org
© 1996 Forest Stewardship Council

Contents

Introduction

Albania is a small, mountainous country stretched along the Mediterranean coast between Montenegro and Greece. For decades Shqipëria, the 'land of the eagles', as the Albanians call their country, was Europe's most isolated and repressive totalitarian state, but now Albania is rapidly becoming one of Europe's most welcoming new destinations. With stunning landscapes, historical towns, world-class excavations and friendly and helpful locals, Albania has a lot to offer the adventurous traveller.

Since the collapse of the totalitarian Communist regime and the ensuing chaos in the 1990s, Albania has changed from a source of emigrants to a stable and booming democracy that has seen constant economic growth for a decade now. Albania is undergoing a true transformation, with construction everywhere, bright new paint, asphalted roads replacing muddy tracks, and ever

Skanderbeg Square in Tirana with its mosque

more facilities for foreign tourists where there were none at all.

Although Albania still is one of Europe's poorest countries, and though much yet has to be done, the country is pleasant, safe, easy and affordable to get around. It must be said that a flexible disposition and travel schedule are necessary to fully enjoy a trip to Albania. Transport timetables don't exist, accommodation standards can be low, sights may be closed when they should be open and road-works may mean long waits or arduous detours to reach your planned destination, but by planning carefully, seeking up-to-date local advice, allowing ample time and by having back-up plans, travellers won't be disappointed.

Myriad sights and experiences await travellers to Albania. Its rich history at the crossroads of European cultures has left the country scattered with ancient Greek and Roman sites, Byzantine churches, Ottoman-era towns, mosques and bridges, and Cold

Alpine scenery in southeastern Albania

War history buffs will stand amazed at the number of bunkers. Albania's landscapes are often spectacular: there's the coast with its picture-perfect sandy coves, wild lagoons and marshes, Arcadian rolling countryside inland, and the brooding mountains, some with dazzling alpine peaks, are always on the horizon.

After decades of neglect, Albania's lively cities and towns are now slowly being rejuvenated and have become pleasant places to spend time, with newly opened parks, renovated monuments, improved infrastructure and many new privately owned hotels, restaurants, bars and cafés. Several malls are now open and more are under construction, and though many products are still imported, it's easy to find great gifts, souvenirs and other bargains. The food is solidly Mediterranean, consisting of simple dishes bursting with fresh ingredients,

delicious seafood, fresh bread and wonderful salads.

Perhaps the most delightful aspect of travel in Albania is the contact with the locals. There are still few Western tourists and most Albanians are delighted to see foreign visitors and eager to strike up conversation – usually followed by offers of coffee or a glass of *raki*, the local firewater. Hospitality is extremely important to Albanians, and especially in more remote areas travellers can encounter disarmingly friendly and generous people. Communication can be hard at times, though with tens of thousands of Albanian emigrants returning home for the summer, an English speaker is never far away.

Whether you come for the beaches or the mountains, for the cultural sights or for the food, you'll be surprised at how easy it is to get in touch with the friendly Albanians and to discover the soul of this enchanting Mediterranean country.

The land

A small country stretched out along the Adriatic and Ionian seas, Albania is only 29,000sq km (11,000sq miles). There are extensive mountain ranges across the country with many peaks over 2,000m (6,500ft). Albania is home to some 3.6 million people, most of them living in the cities after migration from rural areas was forbidden for decades. An unknown number of Albanian emigrants works in Italy, Greece and elsewhere.

The capital city Tirana in central Albania is a true Balkan boomtown: a young and youthful city with grand boulevards, pompous government buildings, dusty side-streets and a scattering of low-key sights. A pleasant day can be spent wandering around the city, visiting the market, having coffee at one of the many cafés or relaxing in

The coast near Vlora

one of the parks. At night, the city livens up, and the streets, restaurants and cafés are packed with families and youngsters.

It's easy to explore central Albania, with the ancient port and seaside city of Durrës just half an hour away from Tirana, and even historical Berat with its Ottoman-era townscape within day-trip distance. Although the area is quite developed and the landscape is merely hilly, these cities should feature in any tour of the country.

Northern Albania has some of Europe's most magnificent mountain landscapes, rivalling the Alps in beauty. The highest peak is Mount Korabi, shared with Macedonia, at 2,764m (9,068ft), though the highest mountain completely within Albania is Mount Jezerca, at 2,694m (8,839ft). Surrounded by these jagged snow-capped peaks, the three main valleys here offer a sense of isolation that is very rare in Europe, with flower-coated meadows, traditional lifestyles (that

TOWN NAMES

You'll see city names spelled in various ways in Albania, for instance Tirana and Tiranë, Shkodra and Shkodër. Albanian words can be both definite or indefinite, depending on their grammatical function within a sentence. To avoid confusion, this guide uses only the definite form (Tirana, Shkodra).

until very recently included blood feuds) and villages dependent on subsistence farming. Set right beside pretty Lake Shkodra, the charming regional capital Shkodra with its mosques, churches and museums is the gateway for the northern mountains.

Inland, southeastern Albania is characterised by yet more impressive mountains: the Gramoz range that rises steeply up to a towering 2,250m (7,380ft), with the fair city of Korça nestled in a high, wide valley. Lake Ohrid, at 690m (2,264ft) above sea level, was formed by tectonic forces millions of years ago, and is one of Europe's oldest and deepest lakes, with many remarkable endemic species inhabiting it, such as the endangered Koran or Ohrid trout. Together with nearby Lake Prespa, the area is well known for its Byzantine cultural heritage in the form of medieval monastery churches, hermit caves and early Christian buildings.

Southern Albania is the focus of many holiday-makers due to what is perhaps Albania's most valuable asset, namely the rugged coastline between Vlora and Saranda with its dazzling bays, marvellous ancient Greek excavations at Butrint and old-world villages where time stands still. Rapidly gaining popularity with holiday-makers from Corfu due to the convenient ferry crossing to Saranda that allows for day trips, the area has seen much investment in tourism infrastructure, yet still is nowhere near the development level of Greece.

Although it is not obvious from driving around the rather barren lower coastal areas, Albania has impressive forest reserves, mainly in the higher and less accessible mountain areas. Despite illegal logging that has caused much damage over the last decade, many forests are in a good state and still support a wide variety of animals, including wild boars, bears and wolves.

A distinct ethnic group, the Albanians look quite different from their neighbours and speak a curious language that belongs to the Indo-European group but is in a branch all of its own. Albania has a quite homogeneous population, with only small numbers of people belonging to minorities, mainly Greeks, Macedonians, Montenegrins and Aromanians. The minorities live in harmony with the Albanian majority, with schooling available in their own languages.

It's also a heart-warming sign that, unlike all its neighbours, Albania is the one Balkan country where Muslims, Bektashi believers, Catholic and Orthodox Christians and atheists all live in peace with each other – and indeed have done so for hundreds of years. Under pressure from a succession of different invaders and occupiers, Albanians have sometimes been forced to change religion for pragmatic reasons, and a popular saying goes, 'the religion of Albania is Albanianism'. In other words, it's more important to be proud of and defend your nation than your religion. Unlike surrounding countries, religion is seldom mixed with politics, and despite continually being branded as a 'Muslim country' in the international press, religion plays a relatively small role in Albania, with only a minority of people regularly visiting churches or mosques. When travelling around Albania, the Catholic and Orthodox believers actually seem more prominent.

With the suppression of the Hoxha years and the chaos following that in the 1990s, Albania has not had an easy time, but as the country is now steadily moving towards becoming a more democratic, stable state, it's increasingly clear that it will emerge as a much more important part of Europe in years to come. Already, the country is a low-cost industrial base for dozens of factories churning out quality shoes, textiles and clothes for export. The food industry is set to follow, now that more canning and processing plants adhering to EU quality standards are being built. Heavy industry and the energy sectors were never well managed, but increasingly foreign firms are entering the market to make the most of Albania's hydropower and mineral resources. The main industry to keep an eye on, however, is tourism, and locals have high hopes that one day soon, booking a beach or mountain holiday to Albania will be as normal as a trip to Italy or Spain.

Typical scenery in the Kelmend Valley

History

7th century BC — Ancient Illyrian speakers, the ancestors of the modern Albanians, settle on the land now known as Albania.

168 BC– AD 395 — The Romans conquer the Illyrians, creating the protectorate of Illyricum until AD 395, when the Roman Empire is divided. Illyricum becomes part of the Byzantine Empire.

1385 — The Ottoman Empire invades. Turkish rule lasts for over 500 years.

1443 — National hero Gjergj Kastrioti (Skanderbeg) (1405–68) launches his revolt against the Ottomans.

19th century — The Ottoman suppression of Albanian autonomy causes intense unrest. With the Ottomans losing ground to the invading Russians in the Balkans, on 10 June 1878, the Prizren League is formed with the purpose of securing autonomy as opposed to Slavic annexation.

1908 — Written Albanian is standardised.

1912 — On the day before the outbreak of the First Balkan War, major unrest breaks out in Albania. On 28 November, Albania declares independence in Vlora.

1913 — On 30 May, the Treaty of London recognises Albanian independence, settling a situation that saw Serbian, Montenegrin and Greek incursions into Albanian territory.

1914 — Italy invades Albania, establishing the Principality of Albania (1914–25).

1925 — Albania becomes a republic. Former Prime Minister Ahmet Zogu (1895–1961) takes office as president on 1 February.

1928 — Ahmet Zogu upgrades Albania to a kingdom and puts himself on its throne as King Zog I.

1939–44 — Italy invades Albania in 1939, overthrowing Zog and occupying the country until 1943. Germany occupies for a further year until partisans force them out. The last Germans leave on 29 November 1944. In May of the same year, the partisan National Liberation Front consolidates Communist rule and makes former French teacher Enver Hoxha prime minister.

1946 Albania becomes the People's Republic of Albania and the first wave of purges begins.

1948 Hoxha cuts all economic ties with former ally Yugoslavia and forms an alliance with Stalin. Albania starts receiving economic aid from the Soviet Union.

1955 On 14 May, Albania becomes a founder-member of the Warsaw Pact.

1960 Hoxha forms closer ties with China, effectively alienating his country from the Soviet Union.

1961 Six years after joining, Albania leaves the Warsaw Pact. The Soviet Union breaks all diplomatic relations with Tirana.

1966 The Albanian version of the Cultural Revolution begins. A violent campaign against all religious organisations is begun. Over 2,000 religious buildings are closed or destroyed.

1978 Following steadily deteriorating relations, China cuts off its aid to Albania.

1985 On 11 April, two days after suffering a heart attack, Enver Hoxha dies.

1992 The Democratic Party wins 62 per cent of the vote. The archaeological site at Butrint is included on the UNESCO World Heritage list.

1993 Pope John Paul II visits.

1997 A state of emergency is declared and 2,000 people lose their lives during the Lottery Uprising (*see p15*).

2003 The first negotiations with the EU begin on Albania's eventual EU membership.

2007 George W Bush visits.

2009 Albania joins NATO.

The Hoxha years

Like other countries with histories of long foreign occupations, Albania's short-lived independence between the two world wars was given a short, sharp slap in the face in the 1940s with the dramatic arrival of Socialism. The individual to make his way to the head of the Albanian Communist table during the turmoil of World War II and to rule the roost for the next four decades was a Gjirokastra-born French teacher, partisan and all-round dictator by the name of Enver Hoxha.

Hoxha (16 October 1908–11 April 1985), the son of a Sunni Muslim cloth merchant, led a life filled with

A bunker from the Communist era near Bajram Curri

many interesting and bizarre twists and turns that would lead him to fame and fortune as Albania's prime minister (1944–54), Minister of Foreign Affairs (1946–53) and, last but not least, the First Secretary of the Communist Party, a position he held until his death in 1985. Politically inspired, at least so the story goes, by his uncle Hysen, a radical Albanian nationalist, and introduced to the writings of Karl Marx when studying at the French Academy in Korça, Hoxha went to France in 1930 and studied briefly at the University of Montpellier before dropping out a year later and moving to Paris. Pausing in the capital just long enough to attend a few lessons at the Sorbonne and write a handful of left-leaning articles on the situation at home, Hoxha's feet were soon itching again, taking him this time to Brussels, where he entered the Albanian diplomatic service. Fired for keeping Marxist literature inside the Albanian embassy (the country was at the time a kingdom), Enver Hoxha returned to Albania in 1936, continuing the same erratic pattern before he opened a tobacco shop in Tirana which soon became a hotbed of Communist activity. It was eventually closed by the occupying Italian fascists.

Elected into the *nomenklatura* of the newly founded Communist Party of Albania, Hoxha rose quickly to the position of first secretary, a position he held for the next 42 years until his death. The aftermath of World War II saw Hoxha cement his position as absolute ruler of Albania, dipping his toe into the camps of Tito, Stalin and Mao along the way before falling out with all of them and forcing Albania into almost total isolation. The head of what was one of the harshest of the many totalitarian regimes of its age, Enver Hoxha created an Albania that was characterised by torture, poverty and, above all, paranoia. His

An Albanian Communist Party mural

own peculiar brand of Stalinism involved turning the country into a fortress, embarking on endless failed industrialisation projects, the banning of religion and, when he didn't get his way entirely, extraordinary acts including the famous incident when he shot a cabinet minister with whom he disagreed. The extreme personality cult that surrounded him continued until his death in 1985, the year Mikhail Gorbachev took control of the Soviet Union and the year that marked the beginning of the end of Communist Europe. Despite the continuing popularity of Socialism in modern Albanian politics, nostalgia for the rule of Enver Hoxha is almost non-existent.

BUNKERS

The Albanian version of the English cartoon featuring a mountain climber reaching a snow-covered summit only to find that someone not just got there before him but also left a shopping trolley behind would undoubtedly feature a concrete bunker instead of a trolley. Between 1950 and 1985, an estimated 800,000 little concrete mushrooms (an amazing one bunker for every four people in the country) were built and placed throughout Albania to deter an invasion that never came. Built in two standard sizes, there's even a story that says Enver Hoxha made their designer stand inside an early prototype while the army fired shells at it to prove its strength. Too expensive to remove, most remain, some of them being turned to uses including love nests for local courting teenagers and even somewhere to house sheep.

Politics

Albanian politics have run the entire gamut over the centuries, from the Roman forum to fascist and Communist dictatorships to the blood feud (see p72). Albania was the last totalitarian Communist regime in Europe to undergo the transition to democracy, and the path of political change in the country has been a long and winding one, full of intrigue, corruption and, at times, despair. The country's impending NATO membership is proof that the tide is turning.

Modern Albania is a parliamentary representative democratic republic complete with a prime minister, who is the head of a government formed by a multi-party system, and a president, elected by parliament through a secret ballot for a term of five years. The current multi-party system replaced the former Communist one-party state in 1991 and is dominated by two parties, namely the centre-right conservative Partia Demokratike e Shqipërisë (Democratic Party of Albania) founded in 1990 and the first legal opposition party in the country, and the leftist Partia Socialiste e Shqipërisë (Socialist Party of Albania).

The last parliamentary elections were held in July 2005. The Democratic Party of Albania won 56 of the 140 contested seats and currently runs the coalition, forming a government with Prime Minister Sali Berisha, the country's former president who served from 1992 until 1997. Bamir Topi is the country's president, having taken office on 24 July 2007. The next scheduled elections are in 2012.

The president performs all major state duties, acts as the head of the armed forces and elects the prime minister. Executive power rests entirely with the cabinet. Ministers are

Some older Albanians still wear the Communist red star

The headquarters of the Socialist Party in Tirana

nominated by the president on the advice of the prime minister. The Kuvendi i Republikës së Shqipërisë (Assembly of the Republic of Albania) passes all Albanian laws. The assembly is made up of 140 deputies, 100 being directly elected by the electorate and 40 by their representative parties on the basis of proportional representation. Parliamentary elections are held every four years at least. The assembly makes all major domestic and foreign policy, including changes to the constitution and the declaration of war on a foreign power or powers. There are no bodies monitoring governmental or parliamentary procedure, and many people believe that Albanian politics is entirely corrupt.

THE LOTTERY UPRISING

In the mid-1990s, the Albanian government endorsed a series of pyramid investment schemes, in which some two-thirds of the population of the country invested. By January 1997, the extraordinary offer of making money that was too good to be true turned out to be just that, and the schemes collapsed with a loss of some £600 million. Blaming the government, who were suspected of profiting from schemes which were in reality fronts for money laundering and arms deals, the people took to the streets demanding their money back in what has become known as the Lottery Uprising. Mass rioting and anarchy ensued, a state of emergency was declared, some 7,000 UN troops were deployed and around 2,000 civilians were killed. The government was eventually toppled and order finally restored.

Culture

Situated at the crossroads of different cultures and lifestyles, Albania's cultural scene is as varied as its history. Every wave of invaders and rulers left its mark on the local population. Now, after decades of isolation, Albanians have been set free and have emigrated en masse, and on visiting Albania you'll find that many new developments are powered by returnees from Greece, Italy, the UK and the USA. Ever-changing, Albania's culture is unique yet recognisably European.

Architecture

Traditional Albanian architecture is best seen in the museum areas of Kruja, Berat and Gjirokastra as well as in Shkodra. The ethnographic museums in each of these centres are housed in 18th- and 19th-century middle or upper class merchant family houses and are well worth a visit. The *oda* room was the most important room: guests were entertained, meals served and the menfolk would sleep here. Separated from the 'public' areas are the *harem* or family rooms. The women and children were kept well out of sight when the men talked business. Some houses have latticed galleries where the women could sit and eavesdrop on the conversations without being seen. Wealthy families would have an in-house *hamam* (bathroom).

Traditional village architecture is quite simple, usually consisting of one-storey stone houses with shingles on the roof. A north Albanian peculiarity is the *kulla* (defence tower), which was used by men targeted during a blood feud. Sometimes incorporated into a farmhouse or else standing free, these towers have no windows on the lower floors and a high entrance with a retractable ladder to block entry to others. Men would spend weeks, months and sometimes years in these dark and dank buildings. A fine example of a free-standing *kulla* can be found in Thethi, but there are many others visible in villages in the north.

'European-style' architecture was late to arrive in Albania, and cities like Tirana and Shkodra have the best examples of modest town houses built in neo-Baroque or similar styles. The Communist period brought little but depressing concrete apartment blocks, but now that the economy is booming, international styles can be seen popping up in cities across the country, with Tirana leading the way. At the moment, various daring modern designs by international architects are under construction.

Decorative arts and handicrafts

Albania is rich in historical artworks, be they Greek statues, medieval early Christian floor mosaics or Byzantine-era icons. The National History Museum in Tirana and the two icon museums in Berat and Korça house perhaps the nation's finest works of art.

Handicrafts such as carved wooden items and copper plates with motifs are for sale at souvenir shops and markets around the country. One modern artist worth remembering is Vangjush Mio (1891–1957) from Korça who studied in Bucharest and Rome and made 700 paintings and sketches, including beautiful city scenes and landscapes and some daring nudes. His Korça house beside the cathedral is a small museum. Tirana has several galleries selling modern works by young Albanian artists.

Literature

It wasn't until medieval times that clergy in Shkodra wrote the first documents in the Albanian language, and it was only in the 19th century that the Albanian national renaissance spawned a generation of writers, poets, politicians and intellectuals. Famous names that are immortalised in street names across the country include Jeronim de Rada, Pashko Vasa, Andon Zako Çajupi, Naim Frashëri, Filip Shiroka, Fan Noli, Gjergj Fushta and Migjeni. For more in-depth information on Albania's writers and poets, visit *www.albanianliterature.net*

Music

Music played a very important role in what was until relatively recently a non-literate country. Songs were the best way to convey historical events and moral codes from generation to generation. Albanian folk music is recognisably Balkan in origin, although it moved away from the Ottoman tradition during the national renaissance years to become more Western. Folk music from the north and the south differs considerably, with the north preferring simple, epic tales of heroism and resistance, or songs with pastoral themes. Traditional northern instruments include the *çifteli*, a lute with one string for the background tone and one for melody, the one-stringed *lahuta* and the *def* drum. In southern Albania, the style is much more romantic and lyrical, with the added speciality of the use of clarinets and polyphonic singing. Despite the long tradition in music, live shows are difficult to find, although major folk festivals are held regularly in Përmet, Peshkopi and Gjirokastra.

Performing arts

With only a short history of stage arts and dramatically underfunded theatres, this branch of art is understandably limited in Albania. Tirana's theatres and Palace of Culture are the best venues (*see p36*), but don't expect English-language performances. Children will love the Tirana Puppet Theatre regardless of the language (*see p131*).

Festivals and events

Apart from the major events listed here, there's no shortage of other interesting events and festivals in Albania, but as most of them are aimed at a local audience, the main problem for foreign visitors is finding out about them in advance. Often you'll only learn about an up-and-coming event when the posters get put up a few weeks or days beforehand, and sometimes the organisers don't even do that. Keep your eyes peeled and ask around for the latest events information when you're in the country.

April

International Festival of Modern and Contemporary Dance, Durrës
Events and workshops by some of the leading dance companies in Europe.
www.dancealbfest.com

Tirana Music Festival
Orchestral and traditional music concerts held in various venues in the last week of April.

Crowds at a Catholic festival in Shkodra

June

Lake Day
Various festivities on both sides of Lake Ohrid, held on 21 June.

Përmeti Multiculturor Folk Festival
Held over four days in late June, the festival brings together groups from across the Balkans and beyond for concerts, book and CD presentations and wild feasting.

July

Butrint International Festival of Theatre
Held in the 2,200-year-old, 700-seat outdoor theatre inside the archaeological site at Butrint (*see pp100–101*), this astonishing event held over one week stages performances from several groundbreaking European theatre companies.
www.butrinti2000.com

Shkodra Jazz Festival
A three-day festival in the city, which has now been running for five years. The growing list of performers

includes top acts from Albania and Italy.

www.shkodrajazz.com

Tirana Jazz Festival

Under the tutelage of its honorary president, the multi-talented German artist Hans-Joachim Roedelius, this peculiar event held over several evenings at the Sheraton hotel offers a wildly eclectic mix of music from a host of international performers.

www.movingculture.org

August

Mount Tomorri Pilgrimage

Throughout August, thousands of Bektashi Muslim believers make the pilgrimage to the shrine high up on Mount Tomorri near Berat to offer sheep and pray in honour of Abbas ibn Ali, victim of the battle of Karbala. Visitors are welcome, though nature-lovers should choose a less busy time to climb the mountain.

Dardha Village Festival

The village is polished and the inhabitants show off their best traditional clothes during the annual festival. There's a crafts market, eating, drinking and plenty of general merrymaking, all on 16 August.

September

Mjaft Fest

Albania's only pop music and youth culture festival is organised in late August or September by the civic society movement Mjaft ('enough'), which battles corruption and political incompetence. The 2007 festival was held on Durrës beach, the 2008 event was in Tirana.

www.mjaftfest.com

International Folk Music Festival, Gjirokastra

Currently held every four years in September in the castle, the last one in 2008, this is one of the finest festivals in the country. The next one is scheduled for 2012, although it's hoped that one will be organised before then, if a budget is found.

www.gjirokastra.org

Peshkopi Folk Festival

A popular two-day festival with handicrafts, exhibitions and Albanian musicians and bands from across the Balkans.

December

Tirana International Film Festival

Held during the first week of the month and featuring a wide range of fiction, documentary, animation and experimental films. Films are screened at the Albanian Art Institute and the Millennium 2 Cinema (*see p144*).

www.tiranafilmfest.com

Mjaft Fest

Nature and wildlife

With humid wetlands along the coast and lakes, dry hilly zones, alpine meadows and rocky mountain peaks, Albania's landscapes and climate zones are so diverse that the country is home to an impressively wide variety of flora and fauna. Although many areas have been subject to human intervention, pollution and other influences in recent years, ecological awareness is slowly growing among the Albanians, who realise the impact of the environment on their lives and the tourism industry. The local flora ranges from Mediterranean to alpine plants, and a few dozen of the over 3,000 species are endemic.

Albania has extensive wetlands, marshes and lagoons along the Adriatic coast, near Butrint and around the big lakes inland. Ideal for bird-watching, many of these areas have watchtowers from which visitors can view the more than 300 species of Albanian birds. Some areas are protected by law, though unfortunately that doesn't necessarily put an end to illegal construction and poaching. These areas are important resting places for migratory birds on their way south or north, and if you time your visit carefully you could well find yourself looking at flocks consisting of thousands of birds. Albania is named after the eagle, but, although you have a chance of spotting one in the wetlands, they are decreasing in number. Dalmatian pelicans can be seen in various places, but it's at Lake Prespa in the southeast that these big birds occur in large numbers. Other birds to watch out for include owls, cormorants, spoonbills, ibises and woodpeckers.

Despite overfishing, Albania's ancient tectonic lakes still support several endemic fish species, such as

Wild flowers in the Valbona Valley

Entering the Llogora National Park

the *koran* or Ohrid trout, found in Lake Ohrid in the east. The unique characteristics of these lakes have also led to the development of various endemic plant species.

At sea, the most common fish are carp, red mullet and sardines. Inland, the lowlands and hills are covered in shrubs and low forests that are well equipped to deal with extended dry periods. Large animals are seldom seen here, but tortoises and other sun-loving reptiles are a common sight, especially in the south.

The isolated mountains of the north and the south of the country are covered with deciduous forests full of beech, oak and other trees, and the hills east of Bajram Curri are well known for their chestnut trees. Higher up the mountains you'll find beautiful

forests of pines and conifers. Deer, wild boar and chamois can be spotted in the forested mountains, for instance at the Llogora Pass or in the forests around Dardha in the southeast. Although Albania has significant numbers of large carnivores such as brown bears, wolves and lynxes, they are seldom seen.

Eco-tourism in Albania is in its infancy, with very little infrastructure, specialised information offices or other initiatives to educate foreign visitors about the local flora and fauna. If you're interested in getting closer to nature, your best bet is to contact **Outdoor Albania** (*see p145*) in Tirana, who can organise short or longer trips with expert guides in the fields of biology, ornithology, forestry and other disciplines.

Highlights

Danilovgrad Lëpusha
MONTE-
NEGRO
Valbona
Erenik
KOSOVO
Kosovo Polje
Janjevo
Tropoja
Orahovac
Gnjilane
Thethi
Bajram Curri
Dakovica
Uroševac
Fierza
Mušutište
Kačanik
Lake Shkodra
Koman
Kukës Dragaš
Tearce
Shiroka **SHKODRA**
Pushë Arës
Bojana-Buna Landscape Park
Vau i Dejës
Tetovo
Skopje
Velipoja
Negotino
Shëngjin
Lezha
Gostivar
Ishull-Lezha
Peshkopi
Adriatic Sea
Laç Burrel
MACEDONIA
Gjiri i Lalëzit
Fushë-Kruja
Kruja
Zajas
Debar
Kičevo
Tirana International Nënë Tereza
Bulqiza
Debrešte
DURRËS
Mount Dajti 1611
Kruševo
Gjiri i Durrësit
TIRANA
Stërbleva
Krivogaštani
Kavaja
Shenenikut 2253
Struga
Demir Hisar
Rrogozhina
ALBANIA
Librazhd
Ohrid
Mogila
Peqin Elbasan
Përrenjas
Resen
Bitola
Cërrik
Lake Ohrid
Bukovo
Lushnja
Kotor
Pogradec
Gramsh
Pogori
Lake Prespa
Florina
Fier Roskovec
Koçova
Vashtëmi
Poljan
Vatohori
Portëz
Berat
Voskopoja
KORÇA
Ballsh
Poliçan
Boboshtica Mborja
Kastoria
Narta Lagoon
Greshica
Çorovoda
Dardha
Argos Orestiko
VLORA
Karaburun Peninsula
Tepelena
Kelçyra
Erseka
Neapoli
Orikum
Përmet
Gëmenj
Eptahori
Ionian Sea
Palasa Dhërmi
Antigonea
Leskovik
Grevena
Spile Palermo
GJIROKASTRA
Konitsa
Piqeras
GREECE
Shën Vasil
Delvina
Saranda
Kakavija
Kalpaki
Ksamil
Metsovo
Corfu
Butrint
Eleousa
Ioannina

① Tirana Albania's relaxed capital has a handful of sights and lively market, but the city is best visited for the lively restaurants and bar scene (*see pp28–36*).

② Kruja An easy half-day trip from Tirana, Kruja is a medieval citadel town that was the base of national hero Skanderbeg (*see p37*).

③ Thethi An isolated mountain village that can only be reached in the summer months, Thethi is well equipped to receive travellers searching for alpine landscapes and good hiking (*see pp66–7*).

④ Lake Koman ferry ride Southern Europe's most spectacular ferry ride links the coastal plains with the Albanian highlands (*see pp64–5*).

⑤ Lake Ohrid The deepest lake in the Balkans and arguably the oldest lake in Europe, Lake Ohrid's neighbouring towns and villages offer the opportunity to base yourself next to a source of water-borne adventures including sailing, fishing and swimming (*see pp80–81*).

⑥ Berat A UNESCO World Heritage Site since July 2008, Berat claims to be the oldest town in Albania and merits at least a day or two exploring its magnificent Ottoman old town and inhabited hill fortress (*see pp48–51*).

⑦ Gjirokastra Yet another World Heritage Site beauty, Gjirokastra has been inhabited since at least the 1st century BC. The birthplace of the dictator Enver Hoxha and the country's most renowned author Ismail Kadare, highlights include the ancient fortress on the hill complete with a USAF reconnaissance plane, captured in 1957 (*see pp104–106*).

⑧ The Riviera Stretching from just north of the Greek border in the south up as far as the port town of Vlora, the so-called Albanian Riviera features a whole host of unspoiled beaches and some truly breathtaking scenery (*see pp90–97*).

⑨ Butrint Discovered less than a century ago, the ancient archaeological site at Butrint is one of the best-preserved examples of its kind in the world. Home to the ancient Greeks, Romans and Venetians to boot, this is well-preserved, UNESCO-listed architecture with a surrounding nature reserve (*see pp100–103*).

⑩ Korça A charming mountain town with a distinct identity, a lively bazaar area and some excellent museums. Nearby, the medieval Mborrja church, the ghost city of Voskopoja and charming Dardha village are all well worth a visit (*see pp75–8*).

Suggested itineraries

Long weekend

If you're planning a short trip to Albania arriving at Tirana's international airport, head to Tirana for a day of wandering around the city, visiting the National History Museum, the central market, Grand Park and the main boulevard before going to the *Bllok* area for dinner and drinks at one of the many quality restaurants and bars. The next day, visit Durrës or Shkodra, both an easy day trip by public transport. In Durrës visit the archaeological museum and the amphitheatre and wander around the centre before heading by taxi to the beach south of town for a fresh seafood dinner. In Shkodra you can visit the mosque, churches, historical museum and Marubi *fototeka* before heading to Rozafa Castle. There may also be time to travel north of Shkodra to see the Ottoman bridge at Mesi. On the last day of your visit, take a taxi or bus to Kruja, where you can see the citadel and have lunch before going directly to the nearby airport. You can also choose to focus on one slightly longer trip out of town, combining a day in Tirana with an overnight trip to Berat in the south where a day suffices to see the main sights and get a good sense of this wonderful town.

If you're arriving in Saranda by ferry from Corfu for a short visit, spend the first afternoon in Saranda, perhaps going to nearby Ksamil for the beaches and seafood restaurants. Plan to spend a full day at Butrint, easily reached by regular city bus, poking around the wonderful ancient ruins in the morning and using the afternoon to explore the adjacent lagoon wetlands using the hiking maps provided locally. With one more day, hop on a bus for the scenic two-hour ride to the UNESCO-listed

The Albanian Riviera coastline

The view from Shkodra's Rozafa Castle over the city, lake and mountains

city of Gjirokastra to visit the bazaar, ethnographic museum and castle before heading back. If you're more of a beach bum, head straight out of Saranda towards the Riviera coast where you can base yourself in Himara to explore the coves, beaches and villages along this stunning stretch of Mediterranean coastline.

One week

With a week in the country, you can hit many of the highlights on a circular route between Tirana and Saranda, even if only using public transport. Going clockwise, travel from Tirana to Berat for a day in the Ottoman town, then continue to Gjirokastra for another day of culture. Then it's on to Saranda, your base for visiting Butrint and perhaps the beaches at Ksamil. Finally, travel up the coastal road, stopping off at Palermo Bay for the fortress and perhaps spending a night or two in a beachside hotel before crossing the Llogora Pass to Vlora, from where you can travel to Tirana in a few hours – with possibly a quick side trip to the ruins at Apollonia. Alternatively, do an inland trip from Tirana that combines Berat with Elbasan, Lake Ohrid and Korça, with an extra excursion to Voskopoja or Dardha in the mountains. North of Tirana, it's easy to spend a week visiting Shkodra, Thethi or Vermoshi in the mountain valleys to the east and Lake Shkodra.

If you arrive in Saranda, you could do a week-long trip of the interior from there, taking in Gjirokastra, the stunning road to Korça with a short visit to Voskopoja or Dardha, and then on via Pogradec and Lake Ohrid to Elbasan, Berat and back to Saranda via Gjirokastra.

Two weeks

With two weeks in Albania you can extend and combine the various circular tours mentioned above in several ways. You could decide to travel the beautiful mountain route between Gjirokastra and Korça, perhaps stopping off at Përmet for the night. Spend a day in Korça for the museums and other sights, and spend a few hours in either Voskopoja or Dardha,

easily visited by car or taxi. Then it's on to Pogradec and Elbasan, skirting Lake Ohrid's southern shores, from where you can pick up the trail at Berat. Whether you're travelling by private or public transport, it's easy to do a two-day detour to lovely Ohrid town on the Macedonian side of the lake before re-entering Albania. Instead of the loop through southeastern Albania, you could choose to venture north, using the charming city of Shkodra as a base to visit Mesi Bridge, Rozafa Castle and Albania's other great shared lake.

In summer, a visit to the mountain village of Thethi is highly recommended for a few days of fresh air and outdoor activities.

Looking across the Ottoman town of Berat towards the mountains

Partisan monument in Pogradec

Longer

If you're lucky enough to have three weeks or more in Albania, you can comfortably cover the whole country, taking in the destinations mentioned above and also visiting some special places well off the beaten track. If you're a hiker, consider hiring a guide and trekking around Thethi, or walking from Thethi over to Valbona in the next valley. You could travel to the isolated Lura National Park for a few peaceful days in the forests, or visit Peshkopi in the east of the country. Further south, you can use Berat as a base to explore the region around Mount Tomorri, or head to Korça to explore fascinating Lake Prespa and the various other day-trip possibilities. To stay closer to the beaches, plan a longer stay in one of the small villages along the Riviera coast to experience the Mediterranean lifestyle – spend a day on the hillsides with a goat shepherd, or help a farmer with the olive harvest for a true taste of rural Albanian life.

HYDROPOWER

With limited oil and gas reserves and plenty of mountainous areas, Albania is highly dependent on hydropower for its energy supply. Apart from the handful of large dams, there are some 80 smaller hydropower plants across the country. Increased energy consumption combined with unreliable rainfall has become a big problem in recent years, with lake levels and electricity production too low to meet even half of national demand at times, resulting in power cuts across the country. A campaign of privatisation, investment in new hydroplants and increased efficiency is now under way.

Tirana and around

Europe's quirkiest capital city may not be packed with sights or brimming with cultural events, but Tirana is well worth visiting. As the political, economic and cultural centre of Albania, Tirana has more and higher quality services than any other Albanian town, and it's here that you'll find the best shops, hotels, restaurants and nightspots. And if you're tired of the busy and dusty city streets, it's easy to escape Tirana on day trips to some great destinations in the area.

Tirana's National History Museum is an essential visit for anyone trying to understand anything about the country, but otherwise Tirana is simply a pleasant city to wander around, with several interesting Ottoman- and Italian-era monuments, charming small markets in dusty residential streets and well-used parks. Boutique shopping is at its best in the Bllok area and along Rruga Myslym Shyri, while elsewhere there are several good art galleries selling works by local artists. In the early evening, families and friends gather in the city centre to stroll around Rinia Park and the newly pedestrianised streets in the Bllok area, chatting, shaking hands and drinking coffee or cocktails at the numerous cafés and bars. Tirana has dozens of good restaurants, serving excellent meals at prices well below Western norms.

Tirana's surroundings offer several worthwhile day trips. The lush forests on Mount Dajti are easily reached with the modern Dajti Ekspres cable car, while the castle at Petrela and the citadel town of Kruja are also just a short drive away.

Tirana
Bllok
Less than 20 years ago, the 'block' area bordered by the Lana River, Rruga Dëshmorët e 4 Shkurtit, Rruga Abdyl Frashëri and Rruga Sami Frashëri was home to Enver Hoxha's party élite and

ADDRESSES

Just because a street exists in Albania doesn't mean it has to have a name, and even if it does have a name it doesn't necessarily follow that anyone knows what the name is. This is the state of affairs throughout more or less the entire country, meaning in short that many places in this guidebook don't have an address listed. Wherever possible we've either included directions on how to get to a place, have marked it on a map, or have assumed that it's so big you can't miss it. The biggest and best resources for all problems large and small in Albania are the people, who will bend over backwards to help an honoured guest in their country.

was strictly out of bounds for normal Albanians. After the revolution, the district with mainly low villas was transformed into the city's new centre, with towering residential buildings, office blocks, restaurants and cafés. At the northern end of Rruga Dëshmorët e 4 Shkurtit, the **Sky Tower** building offers great views over the city centre from its roof top terrace and revolving restaurant, and even if you don't plan to eat or drink there, it's well worth

taking the free elevator up. Nearby, on the corner with Rruga Ismail Qemali, the slightly ramshackle 1970s villa is where dictator Enver Hoxha lived. It's now a government guesthouse. *Rruga Dëshmorët e 4 Shkurtit.*

Galeria e Arteve (Art Gallery)

Besides a good collection of medieval icons and icon screens, Socialist Realism and modern works by local artists, the city's Art Gallery has

Tirana (*walk route on pp32–3*)

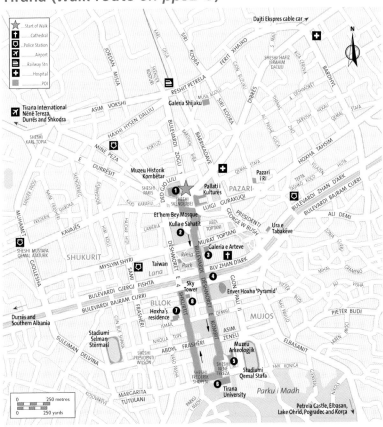

changing exhibitions on various subjects. Walk around the back of the building to find some forgotten Communist statues. There's a lovely garden in front of the gallery.
Blvd Dëshmorët e Kombit.
Tel: (04) 223 3975. Open: Tue–Sun 9am–1pm & 5–8pm. Closed: Mon. Admission charge, but free on Sunday.

Galeria Shijaku (Sali Shijaku House)
One of Tirana's last remaining Ottoman-era houses, the Shijaku with its vine-shaded courtyard café is a fine destination when you're wandering around town. The old house has a large central space displaying the modern works of the owner, Sali Shijaku.
Rruga V Luarasi. Tel: (04) 226 1458. Open: 9am–5pm. Admission charge.

Kalaja e Petreles (Petrela Castle)
Skanderbeg incorporated this dainty hilltop castle just south of Tirana along

Hoxha's villa and the Bllok area seen from the Sky Tower

TIRANA'S COLOURFUL FAÇADES

One of the first things that artist-cum-mayor Edi Rama did when he came to power was to crack open the pots of paint to relieve Tirana from its awful greyness. Buildings across the city were splashed with colour, and the tradition continues with new buildings often being painted in bright though usually less random colours and patterns. Click on 'the city's renaissance' at the municipality website (*www.tirana.gov.al*) to find amazing photos from before and after Tirana's overhaul.

the Elbasan road into his network of fortifications in the 15th century. The semi-ruined building overlooking the village square and the surrounding hills is home to an excellent restaurant.
Petrela. Tel: 069 208 8138. Open: 11.30am–11.30pm. Free admission.

Muzeu Historik Kombëtar (National History Museum)
Albania's best and largest museum starts with a display of magnificent archaeological finds from across the country, and goes on to show medieval Orthodox icons, traditional costumes, and items related to the national uprising against the Ottomans and World War II. A chilling section is devoted to the victims of the Communist dictatorship, with photos and objects from the horrible labour camps. English-language captions are still limited, so it's best to take an Albanian speaker along to make the most of your visit. The museum also has an excellent shop selling traditional souvenirs and books.

Sheshi Skënderbej. Tel: (04) 222 3446. www.albmuseum.com. Open: Tue–Sat 9am–1pm & 5–7pm, Sun 9am–noon & 5–7pm. Closed: Mon. Admission charge.

Parku i Madh (Grand Park)

Tirana's green lungs, and a welcome spot to cool down on a hot day, can be found at the southern end of the main boulevard, situated on a hill beside the artificial Tirana Lake. Along the main path heading to the top of the hill you'll find several monuments and a well-tended Commonwealth war grave with 52 servicemen killed in Albania during World War II. By the lake you'll find some cafés and a pier with boat rental. *Rruga Lek Dukagjini. Open: 24hrs. Free admission.*

Pazari i Ri (Central Market)

Best visited in the morning, Tirana's Central or New Market area is a chaotic warren of streets between flaking old buildings and is a delight to explore. There are different sections for each product, with the fishmongers

The Central Market in Tirana

displaying the fresh catch brought in from Durrës in mounds of ice chippings near the front of the market, butchers hacking away in the meat hall, and stalls selling delicious fruit and vegetables, dried figs and tobacco heaped up in big mounds. *Sheshi Avni Rushemi. Open: 6am–4pm.*

MERCEDESLAND

Until 1991 there were only about 600 cars registered in Albania, with the majority of the population dependent on ramshackle buses or trains if they were allowed to travel around at all. The lifting of restrictions led to a boom of imported cars, with Mercedes the brand of choice. This is not just because it's a symbol of Western technology, but because Mercedes cars are sturdy and durable and have high ground clearance, useful for navigating Albania's woeful roads in the 1990s.

Rinia Park (Youth Park)

This busy city centre park is the focus of the evening *xhiro* when families descend on the green lawns to play, relax and chat. The strange building in the park is the Taiwan entertainment centre, with cafés, restaurants, a bowling centre and casino. In front of it, the lit-up fountain mesmerises children and adults alike. *Blvd Dëshmorët e Kombit.*

Walk: Tirana

This walk through the centre of Tirana takes in the most important sights, with plenty of places along the way to stop off for a coffee or meal.

The route is approximately 3km (2 miles), for which you should allow between one and three hours, depending on the museum visits.

See map on p29 for route.

The walk starts on Sheshi Skënderbej (Skanderbeg Square).

1 Muzeu Historik Kombëtar (National History Museum)

Stand in front of the National History Museum to view the impressive Socialist-era mosaic and the spot where

Hoxha's statue once stood, now irreverently used as a place for children to drive around in electric cars.

Cross over to the semicircular National Bank building overlooking a small park, where Tirana's informal money changers and mobile phone salesmen do their business. Behind the bank, the new Orthodox cathedral is currently under construction. Walk over the pedestrian crossing to the large statue.

2 Skanderbeg statue, Et'hem Bey Mosque and clock tower

The statue of national hero Skanderbeg (*see p37*), with the Et'hem Bey Mosque and the clock tower in the background, is perhaps the best photo opportunity in town. After visiting the mosque, have a quick look at the landmark clock tower, built in the Ottoman era to inform people of the prayer times.

Walk past the elegant government buildings and down the city's main boulevard, Dëshmorët e Kombit, built to impress by the Italians in the 1930s.

Start in front of the National History Museum

The Pyramid along Tirana's main boulevard

3 Rinia Park and Galeria e Arteve

Opposite the green grass of Rinia Park you'll find the Art Gallery fronted by a small park.
Just a little further you'll cross a wide bridge over the Lana River.

4 Lana River and the Pyramid

This small mountain stream can be wild when the snows melt in spring. The area is nicely landscaped, but just a few years ago the river was completely covered with illegal buildings that were demolished to give the city's public spaces back to the Tiranians. Beside the Lana, Tirana's strangest building is the Pyramid, built in the 1980s as a museum to dictator Enver Hoxha. It only functioned as such for a few years before being turned into a cultural centre. Children enjoy sliding down the steep, slippery slopes of the building.
Continuing down the main boulevard with its tall pine trees, you'll pass several
government buildings, the Rogner Europapark hotel and the main exhibition centre before reaching Mother Teresa Square.

5 Sheshi Nënë Tereza

Mother Teresa, an ethnic Albanian, is honoured with a statue beside the Italian-era university building.
Take one of the paths west of the university building which lead up to Tirana's largest city park.

6 Grand Park

This is a pleasant place to rest and have a coffee at one of the cafés overlooking the lake.
Walking back north along Rruga Dëshmorët e 4 Shkurtit, you enter the Bllok area.

7 The Bllok

Crowded with restaurants and cafés, this is the best place for a drink or meal. From the corner of Rruga Ismail Qemali you'll see Enver Hoxha's villa, once the centre of this strictly guarded district.
Walk to the northern end of Rruga Dëshmorët e 4 Shkurtit.

8 Sky Tower

Take the public elevator to the top floor to enjoy views over the route you just walked and the surrounding mountains.
Walk north across the pedestrian bridge and you're back in Rinia Park; 500m (550 yards) straight on is the starting point of the walk.

Walk: Mount Dajti

There's no quicker escape from the city than a trip up to Mount Dajti followed by a refreshing walk in the forests. Although you can drive up, taking the Dajti Ekspres cable car is the best way to reach the mountain.

The walking distance is between 2.5km (1½ miles) and 13km (8 miles). Allow two to six hours for the walk, depending on the route and breaks.

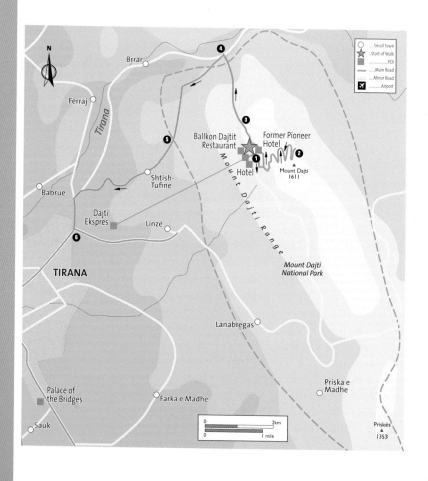

The Dajti Ekspres valley station is located in a suburb of Tirana at the eastern end of Rruga Hoxha Taksim. In operation between 8am and 10pm daily, it takes 15 minutes to whisk you up 800m (2,625ft) to a high plateau beneath the main peak.

1 Cable car top station

Exiting the cable car, walk through the manicured gardens to the edge of the plateau where there are excellent views of Tirana and the wide surroundings as the cable car cabins swing overhead. The adjacent Ballkon Dajtit restaurant is the best place for a meal or drink.
Walk across the clearing and past the car park where the shuttle buses to other restaurants wait. Ahead of you is an old pioneer holiday camp, guarded by vicious dogs. To the left the road goes up to a closed military area. Turn right and follow the road. After passing a derelict house once belonging to Enver Hoxha you'll come to a clearing where the asphalted road turns right. Turn left here and climb up along unmarked footpaths. After entering a forest you'll soon come to a house beside the gravel hairpin road that serpentines up to the top. Follow this road.

2 Mount Dajti peak, 1,611m (5,285ft)

After a while you'll arrive near to the top of the mountain, though you won't be allowed all the way as this is a restricted area due to the many telecommunication installations. On a clear day, there are good views of the city and northwest towards the sea.

Return down the same route if you've had enough or continue as below.

3 Dajti detour

Hiking enthusiasts with a map, good boots and sufficient water can walk all the way down to Tirana. Near the house at the bottom of the hairpin road, look for the narrow asphalted path that heads northwest through lush forest, following the contours of the mountain.
Keep heading northwest before dropping down towards the Tujan Gorge.

4 Shkalle e Tujan gorge

Filled with raging water in spring but otherwise quite calm, the Tujan Gorge is the northernmost point of the walk.
Follow the paths left, or west, down the mountain before branching left.

5 Villages and quarries

You'll leave the forest and pass a village before crossing some barren eroded landscapes and a stone quarry.
The road widens and becomes asphalted near a large cemetery, and after one last hairpin bend you're in Tirana again.

6 Tirana

Here on the fringes of Tirana you'll see the effects that rapid expansion has on a city – what was an area of villages and farmland just over a decade ago is now awash with construction.
It's a few more kilometres southwest to the nearest bus stop on Rruga Dibres, or you can hail a taxi.

Walk: Mount Dajti

Sheshi Skënderbej
(Skanderbeg Square)

Formerly the focus of city life, Tirana's large main square was created by the Italians when they planned their grand boulevard, and later expanded in Communist times. The National History Museum with its striking Socialist façade mosaic stands in front of a pedestal where Enver Hoxha's statue stood until it was toppled in 1991. To the east stands the tall Tirana International hotel and the columned Pallatin e Kulturës (Palace of Culture). The mosque is without doubt the prettiest building on the square. The daintily painted buildings to the south house municipality and ministry offices. The square is soon to be redeveloped into a traffic-free space.

Xhamia e Et'hem Beu
(Et'hem Bey Mosque)

Built between 1794 and 1821, Tirana's pretty main mosque is one of the oldest structures in town. During the atheism campaigns it was turned into a museum, and the reopening of the mosque in 1991 was the first sign of the revolution that eventually toppled the Communists. Decorated inside and out with colourful paintings of famous Ottoman cities and floral motifs, the mosque welcomes visitors to have a look inside, though not during prayer times. Visitors are requested to remove their shoes and to dress modestly, covering legs and shoulders.
Sheshi Skënderbej. Open: summer 8am–10pm; winter 8am–7pm. Free admission.

A sculpture of Skanderbeg and his retinue in Kruja's Skanderbeg Museum

Kruja

High in the mountains north of Tirana, the citadel of Kruja is dramatically set on top of a rocky outcrop with a wall of mountains forming a spectacular backdrop. Easily reached on a half-day trip from Tirana, the citadel is an excellent alternative for time-strapped visitors who can't make it to other historical towns like Berat and Gjirokastra. It's great for shopping, too.

Kruja lies just under 50km (30 miles) from central Tirana and is reached in about one hour by taxi or *furgon* bus. Following signs up the hairpin roads from Fushë-Kruja town via huge dusty stone quarries and lush forest to Kruja's *kalaja* (citadel), you'll arrive at the old bazaar. Consisting of one street with quaint wooden market buildings, this is Albania's prime souvenir shopping mall, with all kinds of gifts and mementos available, including T-shirts, flags, carved wooden objects, copper dishes and antiques.

Walk on and you'll enter the citadel's main gate, opening up to a sloping field with ruins and low buildings. To your left is the **Muzeu Kombëtar Gjergj Kastrioti Skënderbeu (Skanderbeg Museum)** (*open: Tue–Sun 9am–1pm & 4–7pm; closed: Mon; admission charge*), dedicated to Gjergj Kastrioti Skënderbej (*see box*), who was born here and against all odds successfully defended the town many times. History buffs will enjoy the exhibition about Skanderbeg's remarkable life, and there's a good model of the citadel, too.

Nearby, the wonderful **Muzeu Etnografik (Ethnographic Museum)** (*open: Tue–Sun 8am–6pm; admission charge*) is well worth a visit for the lively guided tours alone, where the friendly staff take you on a whirlwind tour of the restored house. The traditional house still retains the separated sections keeping the menfolk and their guests strictly apart from the family rooms, and there's a small in-house *hamam* (bathroom). The streets below this museum lead to a few minor sights, notably the old town *hamam* and the Dollma Teqe, one of the oldest Bektashi temples in Albania (*see pp38–9*).

Finish your visit to Kruja with a meal at one of the small restaurants at the top of the citadel area, each with panoramic views over Kruja and the plains far below. There are several options in the town outside the citadel as well.

SKANDERBEG

Albania's greatest national hero was born as Gjergj Kastrioti in Kruja in 1405. Taken hostage by the sultan at an early age and converted to Islam, Kastrioti fought bravely for the Ottomans, earning the title *Iskender Bey* or Skënderbej (Skanderbeg in English), which refers to Alexander the Great. During a battle in 1443, he defected, eventually making it back to Albania, taking control of Kruja. Using the double-headed eagle as his flag, he forged alliances that would successfully fight the Ottoman army for over 30 years. After many failed attempts, the Ottomans laid on a massive campaign to regain control in Albania in 1467. The following year, Skanderbeg died of malaria while in Lezha.

Religion

Although many people believe that Albania is a Muslim country, it's hard to point at any other country in the region that has such a varied religious scene but without any major conflicts as a result. It was originally a Christian country, but many Albanians converted to Islam after the Ottoman invasion, often for quite pragmatic reasons: taxes were lower for Muslims, for instance. Officially an atheist state between 1967 and 1991, the practice of religion was banned and quite brutally enforced: churches and mosques were destroyed or converted, priests and imams were killed and books and religious artworks were burned. A whole generation grew up without religious education. As a result of these historical events,

72 per cent of the Albanian population is not practising or not religious at all. Whatever the numbers, the popular saying goes that 'the religion of Albania is Albanianism', and it's true that national identity often remains more important than any religious persuasion.

Muslims

Some 21 per cent of Albanians are Muslims, though not usually recognisably so. Beards are rare, as are headscarves for women. Ramadan is adhered to by many people, but the fasting period does not affect daily life at all. After the collapse of Communism, Albania has seen many new mosques built with help from donors from Turkey, Iran and the Arab countries, some projects controversial as they promote a hardline version of Islam that is traditionally absent in Albania.

The Bektashi sect

Seen as heretics by mainstream Muslims, the Bektashi sect is a very liberal branch of Islam that is part of the mystic tradition. Bektashi believers also have one God, revere the Prophet Mohammed and read the Koran, but they incorporate philosophical and

Shkodra's Al Zamil Mosque

Mass inside Shkodra's Catholic cathedral

pagan elements, and also venerate other prophets such as Mohammed's cousin Ali and his two grandsons Hassan and Hussein. Instead of mosques, Bektashis gather at tekkes. Originating in Iran in the 13th century, Bektashism soon spread to Turkey and the Balkans. When Turkey became a secular state in the 1920s, Bektashis were forced to move their headquarters to Albania. Since the return of religious freedom in 1991, many tekkes have been restored and Bektashism is making a slow comeback. If you're in Albania in August, you can witness the important annual pilgrimage at Mount Tomorri near Berat.

Orthodox believers

About 6 per cent of Albanians are Orthodox Christians, with most of them living in the southern half of Albania. Traditionally linked to Byzantine tradition and using Greek during services, the church became autocephalous (independent from the Greek Orthodox Church) in the 1930s. Since then, Mass has been held in Albanian as well as in Greek for the ethnic minority in the south.

Catholics

Although just 3 per cent of Albanians are Catholics, many Catholic believers are concentrated in Shkodra in the north, where it's not unusual to see a priest or nun cycling around town. Shkodra traditionally has had strong links with Catholic Italy since medieval times. The city has the largest church in the Balkans, which was converted to a sports hall in the 1960s, but was reconsecrated in 1991.

Central Albania

Part of the most developed region of Albania, the central area lacks the dramatic mountain landscapes which characterise the north and south, but makes up for this in culture and services. Durrës, Albania's main port, is popular for its long sandy beach but is most visited for the Roman amphitheatre and museum. Inland, Berat is Albania's most charming Ottoman-era town and Elbasan is worth visiting for its bazaar district. Further south along the coast, Apollonia is the region's most important ancient Greek site.

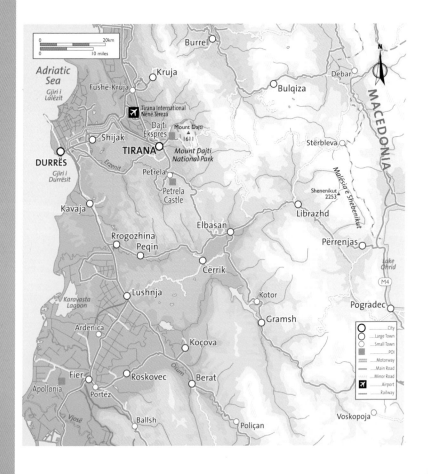

Durrës and its beaches are just 40km (25 miles) from Tirana, and on summer days many Tiranians make the short trip. This is also Albania's main economic corridor, and the area is quickly being developed, with more car showrooms, shopping malls, logistics centres and factories appearing every year. Getting around central Albania is easy, with many public transport links to all cities until late in the afternoon. Buses and *furgon* minibuses ply the Tirana–Durrës route all day long, and this is the one route where taking the train is a reasonable alternative. Apollonia, 90km (56 miles) south of Durrës and stranded in the plains just west of Fier, is a pleasant drive along smooth new highways. If you don't have private transport, a taxi from Fier will be necessary to get you to the site. Berat and Elbasan also have many bus connections with Tirana, the latter best reached by *furgon* minibuses via the mountain road.

DURRËS

Known as Epidamnus to the ancient Greeks and Dyrrachium to the Romans, Durrës is a bustling port where the busy cranes and docks are situated right next to the city centre. The main sights are easily seen in a few hours, and the city is well worth visiting for its historical monuments and for the great evening *xhiro*, when the whole town promenades along Rruga Tregëtare and the seaside boulevard in the evening. Coveted by many due to its deep,

sheltered harbour, Durrës was attacked dozens of times over the millennia, each invader adding to the city's rich history. Indeed, the core of the town is steeped in history, with the top layer of 20th- and 21st-century buildings sheltering medieval Venetian- and Ottoman-era structures that in their turn are built directly on top of ancient Roman ruins. Most locals live in the tatty post-war districts immediately around the old centre, which are gradually being upgraded.

Amfiteatri Romak (Roman Amphitheatre)

The pride of Durrës, the Roman-era amphitheatre on the hillside in the city centre lay buried, forgotten and built upon for hundreds of years until it was accidentally discovered. Now cleared of

Durrës' Archaeological Museum with King Zog's Palace behind

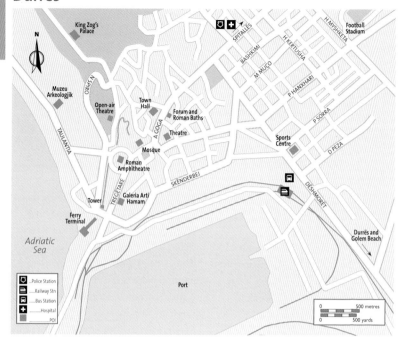

most houses and partly restored, it allows visitors to get a good idea of the magnitude of the stadium that once measured 126m by 106m (413ft by 348ft) and held up to 20,000 people. Some 60 per cent of the original seating slopes are intact, and you can walk through the catacombs once used by gladiators. One of the tunnels holds a 6th-century Christian chapel with wall mosaics depicting Mary, saints and angels.
Durrës city centre. Open: 9am–7pm. Admission charge.

Beaches of Durrës and Golem

The long arc of golden sand lined with hotels that stretches south for several kilometres from Durrës' docks is immensely popular among Albanians, and the short distance to Tirana makes this the beach of choice for refreshment on hot summer days. It's great for a stroll and for the elated atmosphere, but the water quality leaves much to be desired and the beach is often too crowded for comfort. Some 10km (6 miles) south at Golem the beach is slightly less crowded and it's even possible to find quiet stretches backed by trees.

Galeria Arti Hamam (Hamam Art Gallery)

A small Ottoman-era *hamam* (bathhouse) has been restored and now

houses a charming art gallery. The two domed rooms with glass skylights have ornate fireplaces and display art and fascinating old photos of Durrës.
Rruga Tregëtare. Open: 8am–3pm. Free admission.

Muzeu Arkeologjik (Archaeological Museum)

Set in a spacious concrete building north of the centre, Durrës' Archaeological Museum has a good collection of ancient artefacts, though the most spectacular finds from the region are kept in Tirana.

Taking you from the Bronze Age via the Classic era to Roman times, the collection includes delicately carved gravestones, decorative local black-glazed pottery, sacred statues of Aphrodite, lead water pipes and objects found during excavations at the amphitheatre. The importance of sea trade is emphasised with the model of an ancient *anijesh* trade ship and barnacle-encrusted amphorae found on the seabed. There are limited English captions.
Rruga Taulantia. Open: Tue–Sun 9am–3pm. Closed: Mon. Admission charge.

Durrës' Roman Amphitheatre

Via Egnatia

Named after the Roman Proconsul Gaius Ignatius and built in the 2nd century BC soon after the Roman conquest of the Illyrian-speaking lands, the Via Egnatia was a road 2m (6½ft) wide and 1,120km (696 miles) long, used primarily for military purposes and connecting the Roman provinces of Illyricum, Macedonia and Thrace (modern-day Albania, Macedonia (FYROM), Greece and Turkey). Stretching from Dyrrachium (modern-day Durrës) on the Albanian coast and ending in Byzantium (now the Turkish city of Istanbul) on the border between Europe and Asia, the Via Egnatia's journey through what is now Albania left Durrës and followed a route that can still be seen on any modern map, taking in the Albanian towns of Peqin and Elbasan before heading east around the top of Lake Ohrid and out of modern Albanian territory. A secondary part of the Via Egnatia started at the large settlement and trading port at Apollonia before heading north and joining the other route west of Elbasan at Peqin.

One of the most important roads in the Roman Empire, the Via Egnatia brought with it many advantages, opening trade between the East and the West and bringing improved prosperity to the Balkans. Following the old route can be an interesting way of moving between several

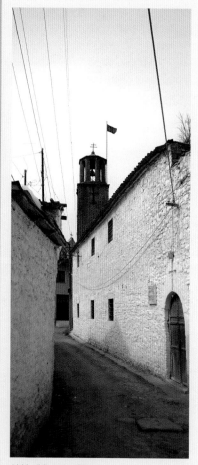

Old buildings in Elbasan

The Via Egnatia started at Durrës' city gates

destinations in this guidebook. In order to get a feel of how life must have been when the Via Egnatia was at its peak, Apollonia (*see p46*) is by far the best place to visit. Not only does it provide an architectural context to the road, the landscape around this part of the coast gives an idea of the strategic importance of both the settlement and the road. The small town of Peqin, or Claudinia as it was known back then, is well off the beaten tourist track, but is worth stopping off at if you're in the area. There's nothing left to speak of from Roman times, but an Ottoman castle still exists. Elbasan (*see pp54–5*), a major fortified town along the Via Egnatia and a few kilometres east of Peqin, offers a crumbling Roman castle inside the Ottoman old bazaar.

THE NEW VIA EGNATIA

Called the New Via Egnatia for the several obvious connections between it and the original, the 670km (416-mile) stretch of fast motorway across Greece from the Turkish border in the east to the Greek port of Igoumenitsa just south of the Albanian border has been under construction for over a decade and is now around 80 per cent complete. Following the original route more or less faithfully from Thessaloniki to Turkey, what's actually called *Egnatia Odos* (the modern Greek translation of Via Egnatia) is interesting for visitors to Albania thinking of driving from Greece. What was once a tedious trip through endless and painfully slow Greek mountain roads with the reward of even worse to come once over the Albanian border has become a much pleasanter option. For progress reports and more about using the road to speed up the journey to Albania, take a look at the road's official website at *www.egnatia.eu*

Walk: Apollonia

Founded by the ancient Greeks in 588 BC, Apollonia was a significant trading port and cultural centre for some 50,000 people before an earthquake in the 3rd century AD forced it into decline. A major centre of Greco-Roman learning, visited by both Julius Caesar and the Emperor Augustus, the site is massive, and relatively untouched.

The walk is relatively short, covering less than 2km (1¼ miles), but will occupy you for a couple of hours.

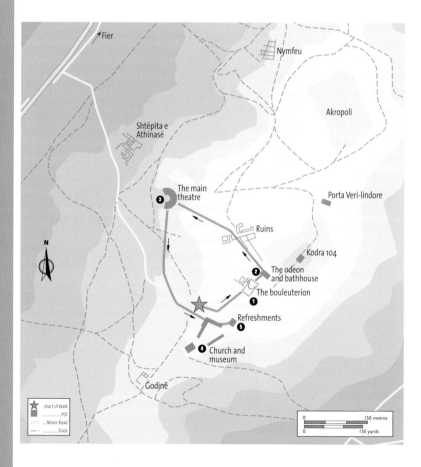

The best way to reach the start of the walk is to drive on the main road west out of the centre of Fier. It's then a long straight drive out of the town (around 5km/ 3 miles) until you see the Apollonia sign. Take the left turn and head down the long straight road, turn left at the end, drive over the river and follow the road round and through what's left of the original city walls to the site car park.

Open: 9am–5pm. Admission charge (church and museum only).

1 The bouleuterion

From the car park, you'll see the Shën Mëri Church to your right, a café in front of you and the main ruins to your left. In front of the church is a small wooden hut, which if open sells a full map of the site. There's also a full site map on a sign by the entrance.

Go through the gate in the direction of the café and turn left. A bouleuterion was an ancient Greek building along the lines of a forum, or citizens' government. Using the original material, some of the 2nd-century BC bouleuterion has been rebuilt, including several of the large, 9m (30ft) columns. Note the application of concrete to the structure, a modern Albanian addition and the cause of much controversy.

Next to the bouleuterion is the recognisable horseshoe shape of a theatre.

2 The odeon and bathhouse

Seating over 500, the odeon has seen extensive renovation work and is occasionally still used for its original purpose. Immediately to the right of it are the foundations of a stoa (a classical Greek colonnade) and a small Roman bath.

Heading northwest past the ruins of another, larger stoa on your right, keep walking down the hill until you reach the ruins of a large, 2nd-century BC theatre.

3 The main theatre

Built to accommodate over 7,000 people, the theatre is indicative of the site in general, being in a poor state and in much need of more renovation work. From this site you can get a good idea of how the city once looked. The view of the sea off in the distance is truly spectacular.

Head up the hill in the direction of the car park and through the entrance to the 13th-century Orthodox Shën Mëri Church and Monastery.

4 Shën Mëri Church and the Apollonia museum

The church has been modified over the centuries, some of it with materials from the Apollonia site. The inside is breathtaking, and includes the official Apollonia museum, which unfortunately remains in Albanian only but is worth a look for its collection of statues from the site.

Head back towards the first sight.

5 Refreshments

Stop off at Apollonia's café for a well-deserved drink before returning to your car.

BERAT

The magnificent fortified castle town of Berat is an absolute must-see. At 2,400 years old, the country's oldest settlement, on the banks of the Osum River, was awarded UNESCO World Heritage status in July 2008, and quite rightly so. It features a rare inhabited citadel, a marvellous icon museum and two exemplary mosques, so that seeing everything in just one day isn't possible. Getting to Berat is easy from the north, with buses and minibuses serving the town from Tirana, Elbasan and the coast. All buses arrive in the town's main square. Arriving from the south remains logistically impossible.

Tourist information

West of Xhamia e Beqarëve (Bachelors' Mosque), the Beratinformation office is the best place in town for maps, information, guided tours and breaks in the nearby Tomorri Massif mountains. You can also rent an mp3 player here with an audio tour of the town's main sights.
Tel: 068 224 1815.
Email: beratinformation@yahoo.com

Kala (Castle)

Almost 200m (656ft) above the town, Berat's huge pre-Roman fortress once contained a total of 42 churches and at least two mosques, although little remains with the exception of several

Berat

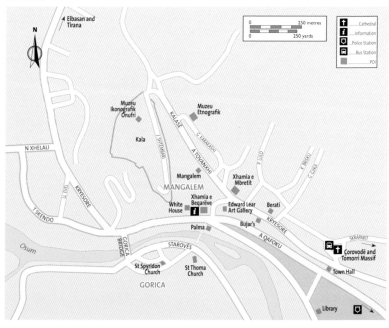

The castle looms high above the town of Berat

Orthodox churches dating from the 13th century. Ransacked by almost everyone throughout its history, including the Romans, Slavs and even the Luftwaffe, the mostly ruined castle is reached up the long steep Kalasë. Entrance is through a large gate that leads to the inhabited part of the complex, and an anti-clockwise tour around the walls guarantees the most impressive experience, not to mention the most exhilarating views of the town and surrounding countryside. Some Orthodox churches are almost intact, although the doors remain firmly locked, their main use now being landmarks for locals stationed around the site and selling the usual tourist tat. The above-mentioned audio tours help untangle what is still a difficult site to understand, although a guided tour is really necessary to get the full impact of

the castle's incredible history. The small restaurant Onufri (*see p146*) near the main entrance serves traditional local food and can get particularly rowdy during the evening. Note that the walk up is hard work. Ask your hotel to call you a taxi if you have any doubts. *Open: 24hrs. Admission charge.*

Muzeu Ikonografik Onufri (Onufri Icon Museum)

The first sight within the castle complex to be made fully accessible to visitors, the Icon Museum is located inside the gorgeous, 18th-century Orthodox St Mary's Church (Kisha e Fjetjes së Shënmërisë). Onufri was a legendary 16th-century Albanian icon painter, famed for radicalising the medium by introducing emotion into the strict codes of Byzantine art. Working throughout the Balkans,

Onufri produced a lot of work in Berat and this small museum features just under 200 exhibits including much of his work plus a few examples of paintings and religious work by other artists. Passing into modern folklore, Onufri's trademark deep red colour is now known as Onufri red.

Open: Tue–Sat 9am–1pm & 4pm–7pm, Sun 9am–2pm. Closed: Mon. Admission charge.

The town centre

All of Berat's main sights are located on the north side of the river. The small park running parallel to Rruga A Qafoku fills during the warmer months with old men in trilby hats playing dominoes and is a pleasant place to relax. The street itself, which is lined with several cafés complete with outdoor seating, is the location of arguably the best *xhiro* in the region. Visiting at around 6pm for the show is a must-see part of any trip to the town. Also worth a mention, the art gallery named in honour of Edward Lear (*see p97*) at the western end of the street features local art plus five prints of paintings of the region executed by the man himself. Despite much Communist-era architectural hooliganism, many of the town's spectacular Ottoman houses remain. One of the simple pleasures of the town is a stroll along its streets.

Muzeu Etnografik (Ethnographic Museum)

Up the hill towards the castle and tucked away to the right, Berat's Ethnographic Museum is located inside a traditional two-floor house. The tour around the building starts with a re-creation of several shops once found in a typical Ottoman-era bazaar, then takes the visitor through a series of rooms typical of a middle-class Albanian household a century or so ago. Notable highlights include examples of how the women were kept apart from the men inside a traditional *mafil* (effectively a prison within the home) whenever guests were in the building, and some really fine carved wooden ceilings. If the door is locked, make yourself known to the security guard, who will go and find someone to let you in.

The King's Mosque is home to some remarkable Ottoman gravestones

Berat's Ethnographic Museum is housed in a traditional building

Open: Tue–Sat 9am–1pm & 4–7pm, Sun 9am–2pm. Closed: Mon. Admission charge.

Xhamia e Beqarëve (Bachelors' Mosque)

Opposite the little footbridge across the river at the western end of Rruga A Qafoku and built in 1827 for the unmarried Muslim male shop assistants, the Bachelors' Mosque is notable for the brightly painted folk motifs on its external walls, very unlike what one ordinarily associates with Islamic art.

Free admission (if you can find someone to open up for you).

Xhamia e Mbretit (King's Mosque)

Dating from the 15th century and found at the bottom of the hill leading up to the castle, the King's Mosque is well worth having a look inside if you can convince somebody to let you in. In remarkably good condition considering what it's been through, of particular note are the intricately carved wooden ceilings. Around the back are several Ottoman gravestones in superb condition. The two white buildings across the garden function as a museum and information centre, with opening times remaining something of a mystery. For more information about the current state of affairs, contact Beratinformation (*see p48*). Note the rather thoughtless addition of the number 3 on the front of the mosque, placed there for the benefit of the aforementioned audio tours. The same fate has befallen most of the main sights in town.

The Ottoman era

The Ottoman Empire was a vast Turkish state covering extensive areas within Europe, Asia and Africa. The empire lasted over 600 years from 1299 until 1923 and was in many ways the Islamic successor to the Byzantine Empire. Like the bordering Russian and Austrian empires, the Ottoman Empire spread a heady infusion of culture and religion, offering security and a civilising influence to a multitude of small nation states in return for a share of their wealth. World War I dealt the final death blow to the Ottoman Empire, which was replaced by the founding of the Republic of Turkey on 29 October 1923, ten years after Albania declared independence in 1913.

During the first half of the 14th century, the Ottomans began their westward expansion, encroaching on the Byzantine lands of Europe. At the time, Albania was little more than a series of squabbling, tribal, Albanian-speaking lands. Thanks to the cunning of the 14th-century Albanian king and ruler of Durrës, Karlo Thopia, who made a personal appeal to the Ottoman sultan to help him conquer his enemy the Albanian-Slavic Basha dynasty, the Ottoman Empire invaded Albania along the Via Egnatia (*see pp44–5*) in 1385, beginning an occupation that was to last into the 20th century.

The leaders of the conquered Albanian clans were allowed relative autonomy in return for recognition of Ottoman supremacy, financial payments and the provision of fighting-age boys into the huge Ottoman army. One such son, Gjergj Kastrioti (1405–68), the youngest of four siblings, served as an Ottoman officer. Later to be known as Skanderbeg, he waged countless wars against the Ottomans and is now considered to be Albania's national hero.

For the most part, however, the empire's softly-softly approach towards Albania had a positive and occasionally bizarre effect. By outwardly converting to Islam, an act that came with all manner of rewards to the convert and his family, the Ottomans inadvertently invented so-called crypto-Catholicism. Out of the home the family would appear by all accounts upholders of the Muslim faith, but at home behind closed doors they would continue their Christian faith. It may be partly because of this that

Ottoman-era town houses in Berat

contemporary Albanians have both an accepting attitude towards organised religion and a healthy contempt for fundamentalism.

Of all the Ottoman rulers of Albania, perhaps none was so famous as Ali Pasha Tepelena (1741–1822, *see p94*), who exemplified the Ottoman Empire. Through the implementation of political strategy and armed conflict, he oversaw the establishment of Islamic culture in the population, constructing mosques and castles, building schools and legal systems, and strengthening the word of Islam and the Ottoman Empire in general. Indeed, the Ottoman occupation of Albania brought much that can still be seen today, including artistic influence, music, food and etiquette. Many Albanians will place a hand on their heart when humbled and will even rock their head in the Asian manner. No other country has quite embraced the Ottoman occupation like Albania and, with the exception of Turkey, nowhere will you find so much Ottoman history and culture left behind.

ELBASAN

A town of just under 90,000 people, Elbasan has until recently been overlooked as a tourist destination thanks to the location of a massive metallurgical complex on its outskirts. Now almost entirely closed down, the plant no longer provides wealth for the population, who are looking at tourism as a way out of the economic doldrums. Home to one of the oldest mosques in the country and boasting a pleasantly laidback feel, a few hours spent in Elbasan are a few well-spent hours indeed.

Elbasan is reachable by bus from just about anywhere of significance in the country as well as being on the rail route from the capital down to Pogradec and Lake Ohrid, so getting there is reasonably straightforward. Those travelling under their own steam either to or from Pogradec and who have the time might like to consider taking the daily train, which passes through some spectacular scenery as well as crossing a handful of hair-raisingly high bridges.

Everything worth seeing in Elbasan is in the centre. Of interest is the old bazaar and castle area, dating from Roman times, but now with Ottoman walls and a surviving Ottoman-era clock tower on its western edge. The bazaar contains Elbasan's two best sights (*see below*), neither of which has specific opening times, but you can try knocking on the doors if they're closed. The area immediately west of the old bazaar entrance features a couple of pleasant parks and the main *xhiro* street (*see p96*). There are no tourist information facilities.

Kisha e Shënmërisë (St Mary's Church)

Located in the eastern half of the old bazaar, the current structure dates from 1833. Inside it's worth a quick look around for the extraordinarily ornate pulpit and a collection of pretty frescoes. In the churchyard is the grave and a small bust of the writer Konstandin Kristoforidhi (1827–95), known for both his contribution to Albanian independence and his efforts to standardise the Albanian language. Kristoforidhi, who was born in Elbasan and who died there after a colourful life abroad and in Tirana, is a national treasure. Another fine statue of him

The statue of Konstandin Kristoforidhi in St Mary's churchyard

The Orthodox Monastery in Ardenica

stands across the street from the southwestern corner of the old bazaar.

Xhamia e Mbretit (King's Mosque)

Work began on the King's Mosque during the same year Columbus sailed for the New World, making it one of the oldest religious buildings in Albania. The witness of many changes since 1492, not much of the original structure survives. There remains confusion about the missing minaret, which according to the imam himself was removed during the height of Enver Hoxha's version of the Cultural Revolution.

ARDENICA

An interesting diversion for those passing through what's otherwise a fairly bleak part of the country, and just off the main road between Fier and Lushnja, is the 18th-century Orthodox Monastery and Kisha e Shënmërisë (Church of St Mary) on top of the hill above the tiny village of Ardenica. The interior of the church is a spectacular masterpiece, featuring a remarkably ornate pulpit and some exceptionally well-preserved frescoes by the famed Zografi brothers, Kostandin and Athanas. From the main road, follow the Ardenica sign up the winding hill for about 2km (1¹/₄ miles). During daylight hours you'll find somebody around to let you in. Admission is free, although spending €1 on the English brochure is well worth the expense.

Northern Albania

Rugged snow-clad alpine peaks, lush green valleys, sparkling lakes, wetlands full of wildlife, long sandy beaches, welcoming traditional villages and historical cities – northern Albania ticks all the boxes necessary for a varied trip. Still, it's largely shunned by foreign travellers who cross the border here but generally spend only a few hours in Shkodra before speeding south to Tirana. However, with some planning, even the wildest corners of Albania can easily be tamed and enjoyed.

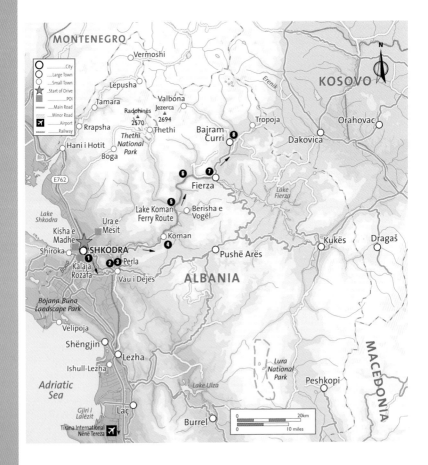

Just 87km (54 miles) or two hours over good roads from Tirana, or an hour from Podgorica or Ulcinj in Montenegro, the regional capital Shkodra is a good base for any exploration of northern Albania. With good hotels, restaurants and other facilities, it's also the regional transport hub. Just west of the city lies Lake Shkodra and the Buna River with their small fishing villages and rich wetland areas. The popular beach destinations along the coast get very busy in summer and the litter and chaos may be overwhelming for some, but it's possible to find more isolated and quiet beaches too. Northern Albania really impresses with its mountainous interior. Albania's highest peaks can be found here, as well as dozens of lower peaks that look no less impressive. With

MOTHER TERESA

The nun known world-wide as Mother Teresa was born in 1910 into a Catholic family originating from Shkodra. She was born as Agnes Gonxha Bojaxhiu in Skopje, capital of what is now Macedonia. Interested in missionary work from very early on, Agnes left home at 18 to become a nun. In Ireland she learned English and then was sent to India, where she would later found her Missionaries of Charity in an attempt to help the poor and sick. She received the Nobel Peace Prize in 1979 and died in 1997. Now the most famous Albanian, Nënë Tereza, as she is known locally, is honoured with statues in Tirana and Shkodra.

good preparation, hiking is a delight here, and even if you don't plan to romp around between the high peaks, you can experience true Albanian hospitality in the small traditional villages hidden in the deep valleys.

Shkodra's Orthodox cathedral

SHKODRA AND LAKE SHKODRA

A pleasant city that lacks the frenetic pace and volume of Tirana, Shkodra is regarded as a centre of culture by Albanians. It's in this dignified old trading city that national writers and poets were based, songs were composed and border politics were discussed by diplomats after the collapse of the Ottoman Empire. The city centre may be small, but there's enough to keep you busy for a day or two, especially if you venture out into the surroundings, with Lake Shkodra as the highlight of any day trip.

You might come away with the impression that Shkodra is a city of bicycles and birds. The flat geography is ideal for pedalling around town, and you'll see many locals doing just that. The accompanying soundtrack to many city streets is that of birdsong – locals hang their cages with songbirds outside so everybody can enjoy their twittering contests. All this contributes to Shkodra's very relaxed atmosphere, though the pace may be set to change a little. After decades of neglect, Shkodra has just recently started a campaign to modernise. New asphalt and street lights, painted buildings, renovated city parks and even bicycle paths have been added, greatly improving the city, which has in the past seemed rather grey and run-down. It's the perfect base to explore the marvellous north.

Tourist information

The main tourism office inside the Rozafa hotel can help with basic questions and brochures. For specific requests about travel to Thethi and Vermoshi, contact **GTZ**, an organisation that is helping to develop responsible tourism throughout the

Cyclists on Shkodra's renovated main street

View of Rozafa Castle across the Buna River

region. A useful downloadable city guide and map of Shkodra can be found at *www.inyourpocket.com* GTZ. Tel: (022) 489 14. Email: gtz_shkodra@yahoo.com. *Tourist Information Office. Rozafa, Rruga Teuta. Tel: (022) 359 0. Email: promovimi.turistik.shkoder@yahoo.com. Open: 7am–3pm & 7–8pm.*

Shkodra
Fototeka Marubi
(Marubi Photo Collection)

The three generations of the Marubi family started taking photos of Albania and its inhabitants in 1858 and built up a carefully documented collection of 150,000 negatives. Now owned by the state and complemented with several other collections, the *fototeka* displays the best photos in its small exhibition as it waits for better housing. It's

recommended to announce your visit in advance.
Rruga Dr Selandin Bekreshi.
Tel: (022) 434 67. Open: Mon–Fri 8am–4pm. Closed: Sat & Sun.
Admission charge.

THE ROZAFA LEGEND

The legend linked to Rozafa Castle says that three brothers working on the construction of the walls discovered that their hard work was undone overnight. Told by a savant that a human sacrifice was required to stop this, they agreed that the first of their wives to bring their lunch up to the castle would be immured in the wall. The two elder brothers warned their wives to stay home, so it was beautiful Rozafa, the wife of the youngest brother, who arrived first. On the condition that a hole was left so she could still touch and breastfeed her baby boy, she agreed to be incorporated in the castle. The castle was finished soon after, but the drops of water that still emerge from the old walls are said to be her tears.

Gjuhadol district

A short walk along Rruga Kolë Idromeno and Rruga Gjuhadol in the city centre leads past Shkodra's most elegant town houses. Recently restored and repainted, the houses date from around 1900 and have many elegant details.

Kalaja Rozafa (Rozafa Castle)

Shkodra's pride is the massive citadel complex perched on top of a hill at the southern end of town. Used as a fortress since the Bronze Age, the walls and buildings currently visible date from the Illyrian, Venetian and Ottoman periods.

Sunset over Lake Shkodra

After passing two sets of gates and courtyards you'll see the ruins of St Stephen, a 13th-century church that was turned into a mosque after the Ottomans invaded in 1479. The third and last courtyard offers great views over the river and holds a Venetian arsenal building with a small museum. *Follow signs to 'Parku Arkeologjik Shkodër'. www.archeologicalshkodra.com. Open: daily May–Oct 8am–10pm; Nov–Apr 8am–5pm. Admission charge.*

Kisha e Madhe (Cathedral)
The large neo-Baroque Catholic cathedral at the eastern end of Rruga Gjuhadol was built in the 19th century. After the atheism campaign of 1967 it was turned into a sports stadium but after the end of Communist rule in 1991 it was inaugurated by Mother Teresa. *Rruga Marin Biçikemi. Open: daily.*

Ura e Mesit (Mesi Bridge)
Albania's best-preserved Ottoman bridge is over 100m (330ft) long and spans the Kiri River with 12 small arches and one elegant large arch. The adjacent modern bridge offers good views of the structure and the mountains beyond. It's best seen in spring when the river below is full and bright blue. *6km (4 miles) north of Shkodra.*

Lake Shkodra
The lake to the west of Shkodra is a good place for a relaxed meal, a day at the beach or a trip on the water. The largest lake in the Balkans, it's shared with the Montenegrins, who call it Skadar Lake. Originally a bay, it was cut off from the sea long ago and the water level and surface area of the lake now vary dramatically with the seasons. Go down the wooden bridge crossing the Buna, the river that flows from the lake to the Adriatic Sea, and turn right to follow the road to reach the villages of Shiroka (after 3km/2 miles) and Zogaj (after 9km/6 miles), at the foot of steep Mount Tarabosh on the southern lakeside. After Shiroka, which looks quite modern with its promenade and lakeside restaurants, the road narrows and enters a wilder area. At the end of the road, Zogaj is a wonderfully authentic fishing village with cobbled streets, olive trees and orchards, stone houses, a mosque and fishermen repairing their nets by the road. It's possible to stay the night here in simple guesthouses with traditional home cooking. Several good restaurants along the Zogaj road serve fresh fish from the lake, of which Taverna Shkodrana is the most popular. There are also a few small coves with gravel beaches where you can relax and swim in the cool, clear waters.

The eastern lake-shore, north of Shkodra, is quite different. Agricultural land borders a wide strip of marshland and reed, providing little opportunity to reach the water, though this part of the lake is perfect for fishing and birdspotting. The Xhenis travel agency inside Shkodra's Europa Grand Hotel has a boat that can be booked for trips on the lake.

Italy and Albania

The long queues for visas at the Italian embassy and consulates show how important Italy is for thousands of Albanians travelling and working there. Although Greece is currently the country's main investor, Italy has historically been close to Albania. Cultural links date back to medieval times, when Italian priests were active in the northern Catholic areas, and Shkodra was long known under its Italian name Scutari. It was, however, in the period after World War I that Italy's influence increased dramatically.

President (later King) Zog of Albania looked to Italy for financial and practical aid necessary for the modernisation of the country. As Italy was looking to reinforce its position in Albania, money and manpower soon flowed in to help drain the malarial coastal marshes and turn them into agricultural land and to construct Albania's first proper roads and bridges. Thousands of Italians settled in Albania, and Italian architects transformed the sleepy bazaar town of Tirana into something more resembling a capital city by building Skanderbeg Square and the system of radial boulevards, hotels, the university and government buildings.

In the 1930s, Albania's dependence on Italy and the risk of losing autonomy became apparent, but after a few half-hearted measures on the part of the Albanian monarchy to establish a more independent Albania, relations were again strengthened. By 1939, Albania was practically a part of Italy, and Mussolini completed the takeover by invading on 25 March and disposing of King Zog, later dragging Albania into World War II when he used the country to invade Greece (*see box opposite*). After the war, Enver Hoxha's Stalinist rule

Tirana's Italian-built ministry buildings

King Zog's Italian-built palace in Durrës

prevented all contact, but soon after the reopening of the borders in 1991, Italy coordinated the EU aid missions to Albania and also became the main target of tens of thousands of economic refugees. In Shkodra and elsewhere, the Italian Catholic Church sent aid and missionaries, and helped renovate and rebuild churches and monasteries.

Italian investors are very important for Albania, and the Italian national and regional governments are major sponsors of aid projects across the country. With Italian radio and TV received in most places, Italian is spoken by many Albanians. Apart from employing many thousands of emigrant Albanians, Italy also is home to the Albanian-speaking Arbëreshë minority, who fled there during the Ottoman invasion of Albania in the 15th century.

THE GREEK–ITALIAN WAR

As World War II progressed, Mussolini grew increasingly jealous of the Nazi victories. Several army divisions posted in southern Albania invaded Greece on 28 October 1940, but from the very start the Italian campaign was dogged by bad planning and insufficient troops. The Greeks had fair warning of the attack and were prepared. Bad weather caused delays on the muddy roads, prevented air support and caused miserable conditions in the mountainous interior. After initial success, the Greek counter-attack drove the Italians back across the border and deep into Albania, where a stable front emerged. The Italians were eventually saved complete humiliation by the German invasion of Greece. Italy's botched operation, which cost the lives of over 60,000 Italians and 13,000 Greeks, is dramatically described in *Captain Corelli's Mandolin* by Louis de Bernières.

Drive: Lake Koman ferry route

The road from Shkodra inland to Bajram Curri and on to Kosovo is so mountainous that it's much quicker to take a ferry along the artificial Lake Koman. Passing through high gorges and sailing by isolated farmhouses and villages, this is the most scenic ferry trip in southern Europe.

Shkodra to Bajram Curri is 133km (83 miles) of which 43km (27 miles) is by ferry. Allow six hours for the whole trip. Find the drive map on p56.

The car ferry from Koman departs at 10.30am, arriving in Fierza two hours later. The ferry back to Koman departs at 7am. From June to mid-October an extra service departs Koman at 3.30pm; the ferry in the other direction departs at 1pm. A daily passenger ferry stopping off at farms and villages leaves Koman at 9am; it sails back at 6am. Food and drinks are available on board. It's essential to arrive at least an hour before departure. Confirm sailing times by telephone (tel: 069 295 4364, Albanian and German spoken). Daily furgon buses between Bajram Curri and Tirana make use of the ferry as well.

Depart Shkodra on time for the 90-minute, 70km (43-mile) drive via Vau i Dejës to Koman. Aim to arrive at least an hour before the ferry departs.

1 Shkodra

After leaving Shkodra you'll cross the plains of the Kiri and Drini rivers, a Catholic area where you'll have a good chance of seeing women wearing traditional costume.
Continue on to Vau i Dejës.

2 Vau i Dejës

Passing through this modern town, look left to see the large dam holding back the huge Vau i Dejës reservoir.

On board the Lake Koman ferry

Initially, you should follow signs towards Puka but as the road to Koman is not indicated, make sure you turn left at a hairpin bend with a sign pointing to the Perla restaurant.

3 Perla

The newly built lakeside Perla complex is a good place to stop for drinks or a meal – it's the last opportunity before boarding the ferry. There are hotel rooms too, if you're looking for a good place to start or end.

Follow the road as it twists high above the lake until you reach Koman.

4 Koman

Here is where all traffic bound for the ferry is stopped in the valley. As all traffic has to go up a narrow road and through a long and winding tunnel, nobody is allowed up until all the cars coming off the ferry have made it down. The second of the three huge dams in the Drini Valley can be seen holding back Lake Koman at the end of the valley.

Driving onto the ferry can be quite an adventure – cars are squeezed into every available space, and even onto the loading ramps. Upstairs you can sit in the smoky café or on the top deck to admire the views.

5 Berisha e Vogël

Half way between Koman and Fierza, near a small island with a cross on it, the lake widens and the small village of Berisha e Vogël appears on the southern shore. Look out for the novel ferry that the villagers use to cross to the other side – an old city bus welded onto a boat.

The ferry continues past more dramatic rock formations before affording a view of Mount Jezerca.

6 Mount Jezerca view

You'll be able to spot the snow-capped peak of Mount Jezerca (2,694m/8,839ft), north Albania's highest peak.

The ferry continues on to Fierza where it stops.

7 Fierza

You disembark onto Fierza's messy provisional pier. Fierza, an equally messy town a few kilometres away, does not merit a stop.

Follow the gravel road for a few kilometres before reaching the asphalted main road that leads up to Bajram Curri and Kosovo. After just 20km (12½ miles) over good roads, you'll reach Bajram Curri.

8 Bajram Curri

The quirky mountain town of Bajram Curri consists mainly of concrete blocks plonked on a hillside. The small town is laid-back and traditional, with mainly men on the streets in the evening. As a foreigner, you'll get plenty of curious looks as you wander along the evening *xhiro* with the locals.

From here you can drive up to the Valbona Valley or head east over newly made roads into Kosovo.

THETHI AND VERMOSHI

A trip to the mountain villages of Thethi and Vermoshi in the high north is perhaps the most adventurous trip available in Albania, even if you don't plan to hike around. These are some of the most isolated communities in Europe, with a long history of lawlessness, blood feuds and emigration. Stability has now come to the area, and the heartwarmingly friendly locals are delighted to welcome visitors to their villages.

Thethi is accessed via Boga village, across a high mountain pass that is unsuitable for normal cars and is blocked with snow between November and mid-May (the alternative route marked on some maps is atrocious but may be upgraded soon). The stunning Kelmend Valley road leading to Vermoshi is normally open year-round, though in adverse weather, landslides and snow may cause problems. In dry weather, experienced drivers can just about make it all the way to Vermoshi with a normal car, but driving a 4WD is a better idea. There's a daily *furgon* minibus to Vermoshi and occasionally one to Thethi; GTZ in Shkodra (*see pp58–9*) will have up-to-date details. Renting a 4WD car with a driver is a safe and much more comfortable way to arrive; count on paying about 12,400 lekë for the bone-shaking four- or five-hour trip to each village. Note that only basic articles are available in the village shops, so bring all essential items with you.

Thethi

The stuff of legend, Thethi is one of Albania's prettiest places: a green valley with widely dispersed traditional farmhouses surrounded by dramatic snow-capped alpine peaks. Thethi offers fine hiking and a million great places to sit down and read Edith Durham's book *High Albania*. There are several guesthouses in Thethi that provide simple lodging and three meals a day. A project to mark the walks around the valley is currently under way, but you can also hire a local lad to guide you around for the day.

In the village centre there's a Catholic church dating from the 19th century. Nearby stands a recently renovated *kulla* or defence tower, used by individuals who 'owed blood' in a blood feud between rival clans. An old building nearby is set to reopen as an ethnographic museum one day. You can

Thethi village in its picturesque valley

A traditional farmhouse in Vermoshi

freely wander around the flat valley floor, or hike up to nearby sights (*see pp68–9*). With a guide or by following trail markings, it's possible to walk across to Valbona in the next valley in about seven hours.

Vermoshi

Getting to Vermoshi involves crossing two passes and driving through the magnificent Kelmend Valley. After climbing up from Hani i Hotit along Lake Shkodra towards Rrapsha, a fantastic valley panorama opens up from the first pass, with fold after fold of rock to the north and the gravel road zigzagging steeply down in dozens of hairpin bends. After passing Tamara, where some farms across the gorge can only be reached in small carts hanging from cables, the landscape becomes even wilder, with the dusty road climbing up through huge rockfalls. After driving through the forests of Selc

you cross the second pass and descend to Vermoshi via Lëpusha village. Both these villages have guesthouses in local farms, and you can expect to share the farm with a multitude of animals.

EDITH DURHAM

The name Edith Durham (1863–1944) is synonymous with Albania. Born in London into a well-off, middle-class Victorian family, and a hugely talented artist, Edith studied at the Royal College of Arts, unlike most other girls of her time and station, and embarked on a successful career as an illustrator. At the age of 37 and still unmarried, Edith fell ill and on the advice of her doctor took what was to become the first of many trips to the Balkans. For the next few years she travelled extensively in some of the remotest parts of northern Albania, recording everything she saw, getting actively involved in the emerging independence movement and meeting several sworn virgins (*see p73*) along the way. Her legacy can be seen in some of the country's street names as well as several fascinating books she wrote about her travels, of which her classic from 1909, *High Albania*, remains in print.

Walk: Thethi Valley

This relatively easy walk takes in the main sights of the valley.

The short walk is approximately 14km (8½ miles), the extended walk 21km (13 miles). Allow at least half a day for the short walk and a full day for the longer version. Bring a packed lunch and water from the guesthouse.

Start in the centre of Thethi.

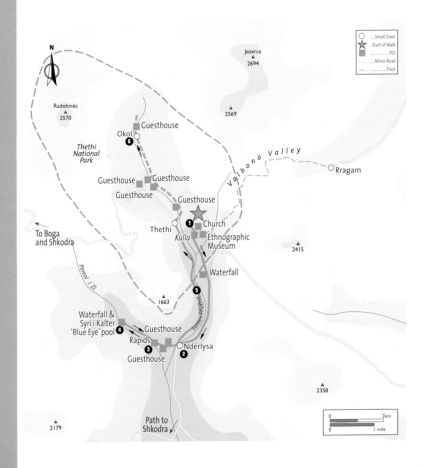

1 Thethi village centre

In the village centre, ask for the keys to the church and the nearby defence tower. Both are worth a quick peek inside.
Follow the marked path below the kulla, keeping the wild Lumi i Thethit River to your right, crossing a side river and continuing along an irrigation channel. After half an hour you can scramble up a marked path to an impressive waterfall. Continue down where a new bridge spans the gorge to the main road.

The rapids at Thethi

2 Bridge

Bridges in mountain communities are of vital importance for transport links but are under threat of being washed away each spring when the snows melt.
Walk west between the farmhouses towards the side valley. After a short while you'll reach the clear blue Perroi i Zi River. Follow this upstream and you'll soon arrive at the rapids.

3 Rapids

Here the water roars through narrow openings between strangely eroded stones. Although the locals enjoy jumping across, realise that falling in

the river here probably means the end.
Follow the path for another 1km (²⁄₃ mile).

4 Waterfall

This high waterfall has created a large pool named Syri i Kalter or 'Blue Eye' after the colour of the water. The pool is great for a dip on a hot day.
Retrace your steps to the bridge and follow the main road back towards Thethi on the western bank of the river.

5 Bridge

You'll have good views of the village and the surrounding mountains from this bridge over the river. Cross back towards Thethi village centre.
If you're up for more, turn left and follow the river further upstream, passing more farmhouses. After a few kilometres, you'll reach the Okol area at the top of the valley.

6 Okol

Surrounded by forests and steep mountains, this feels like the end of the world. There's a guesthouse here that should be able to serve some drinks.
Return to Thethi via the same road.

BALKANS PEACE PARK

Thethi, Vermoshi and the surrounding valleys are all part of the Balkans Peace Park Project, an effort to unite the adjoining mountain areas of Albania, Montenegro and Kosovo into one transnational park. The BPPP works to promote the area to visitors from abroad and to create local jobs while protecting the environment and local culture. For more information see *www.balkanspeacepark.org*

LEZHA AND THE NORTH COAST
Lezha

A historical town placed between Tirana and Shkodra, Lezha is best known for the grave of Skanderbeg, Albania's national hero. The impressive hilltop castle dominating the town is the old Illyrian city of Lissus, which has been added to by virtually every invader since it was built 2,400 years ago. Unfortunately, the castle is not as easy to reach and explore as the one in Shkodra and you'll need to wear good shoes and trousers.

Skanderbeg's grave

The original 14th-century Katedralës e Shën Kollit (St Nicholas Cathedral) that held Skanderbeg's grave on this spot was converted into a mosque after the

Skanderbeg's grave and the castle at Lezha

Ottomans finally took power, and Skanderbeg's remains were destroyed. After independence the church and grave were restored but were then destroyed by an earthquake. The partially rebuilt structure is now protected by a concrete roof. If you find the site closed when it shouldn't be, you can slip through a hole in the gate beside the library to get closer. *Lezha town centre. Open: 8am–7pm. Admission charge.*

Ishull-Lezha

The village of Ishull-Lezha, a ten-minute drive down the Tirana road from Lezha, has several good accommodation and dining options and is a great place to escape the crowds and the traffic. Situated in the marshlands surrounding the old Drini Delta, there's good birdwatching and hunting around protected Lake Vaini (*small admission charge*) and there's a pretty but trash-strewn beach just beyond the lake. Following the asphalt road into Ishull-Lezha till the end, you'll arrive at the depressingly ramshackle 1930s wooden hunting lodge built for Count Ciano, Mussolini's son-in-law and Italy's wartime foreign minister.

Shëngjin

The only harbour town in the north and a major seaside resort, Shëngjin is just 7km (4½ miles) from Lezha with regular *furgon* minibuses plying the route. The town has a bustling port

The beach at Shëngjin

(fish destined for Kosovo is landed here every morning), a military base and a rapidly expanding beachfront with high-rise hotels and apartment complexes. The wide sandy beach stretches south for miles and is backed by trees and the occasional restaurant. The further you get from the town, the quieter and cleaner the beach becomes.

Velipoja

This beach resort closest to Shkodra, 28km (17 miles) away and reached by regular *furgon* minibuses in summer, offers a mix of hedonism and escapism. Unchecked development has led to the construction of many hotels, restaurants and bars along the sandy beach, which together with the lack of parking rules leads to an enjoyable chaos. The festive atmosphere on the beach contrasts nicely with the serene peace that can be found just to the west, in the **Bojana-Buna Landscape Park**. This nature reserve around the arms of the Buna River consists of pine forest, marshland, lagoons and shifting sandbanks, and is home to a wide variety of wildlife, with observation towers provided for viewing. At the end of the path lies a deserted beach with views over to Montenegro. The reservation is reached via a gate near the entrance of the village, or from the beach.
Small admission charge.

KOSOVO

The newly independent province of Serbia, with its 90 per cent ethnic Albanian population, was separated from Albania by Hoxha's impermeable border for decades. Kosovars speak the same dialect as in northern Albania, but the decades of separation have ensured the countries have developed in different ways. During the Kosovo conflict, thousands of fleeing Kosovar refugees headed for Albania. The town of Kukës in eastern Albania, in particular, did an admirable job housing thousands of refugees. With independence and open borders, trade and traffic has picked up enormously between the countries, though the long drive from Tirana to Pristina across the mountain roads remains daunting.

Blood feuds and sworn virgins

Centuries of isolation, poverty, lack of state supervision and the clan-based patriarchal society with its strict emphasis on honour has resulted in some unusual social phenomena in the northern Albanian highlands and mountain areas. Although not unique to Albania, the tradition of blood feuds was strongest here. In the absence of state regulations and justice, offences in the remote areas of north Albania, Kosovo and Montenegro were solved by applying the strict rules written in the *Kanun of Lek Dukagjini*, an ancient text describing all the customs and rules.

The *kulla* tower at Thethi

Men guilty of killing were said to 'owe blood' to the clan of the victim, who in turn were obliged by the *kanun* to take revenge by killing the offender or any of his male relatives (women and children were of little importance). Refusal to perform the revenge killing would lead to the loss of honour for the whole extended clan, a matter of extreme importance. Of course, a revenge killing would ensure that now the original victim's clan owed blood, and the two clans would end up locked in a bitter cycle of rivalry and killings that could last for years, sometimes decades. The men 'owing blood' could retreat into their fortified houses or to a dedicated *kulla*, a special defence tower, to escape from revenge while the women of the clan had to take over the business of farming the land and bringing food to the trapped men. It's estimated that until a century ago up to 30 per cent of all men here came to their end in revenge killings. The killings could be stopped by pronouncing a *besa*, a sworn oath that was sealed by a marriage or payment between warring clans. Although attempts have been made to put an end to the killings since the 1920s, they

A farmhouse with a modernised *kulla* tower in the Valbona Valley

continued after the Communist repression was ended in 1991.

Another intriguing phenomenon linked to the code of honour in this male-based society is that of the sworn virgins. Normally, the death of a male head of a family with no male successors would lead to the family being absorbed into a related family, as a female-only household was unheard of. The one exception to this rule is if a women 'becomes' a man by using men's clothes and habits, cutting her hair short, by doing men's jobs and by promising not to marry or bear children. Unlike other women, these so-called sworn virgins smoke, drink, drive, carry guns and attend village meetings like any man. The sworn virgins are not seen as freaks, and sexuality has nothing at all to do with their actions: they are completely accepted and respected for taking a serious decision that will preserve their honour and allow them to take care of their family. Although many Albanians are unaware of the fact, there are still several sworn virgins in the north of the country, several of them even living in towns and cities.

For further reading, the *Kanun of Lek Dukagjini* is available in English translation at Tirana's Adrion bookshop, Ismail Kadare's novel *Broken April* gives a good insight into the tradition of revenge killings, and Antonia Young's *Women Who Become Men* is an in-depth study of the phenomenon of sworn virgins.

Southeastern Albania

At times unmistakably Albanian and at others decidedly Greek, the southeastern region of Albania is more than a melting pot of ethnicity. Its main city, Korça, is a centre of high culture and home to a bilingual population. Also a blissful retreat from the scorching summer sun, Korça's high altitude makes it one of the coolest destinations in the country. Don't miss its bustling bazaar or the magnificent 13th-century Kisha e Mborjes church.

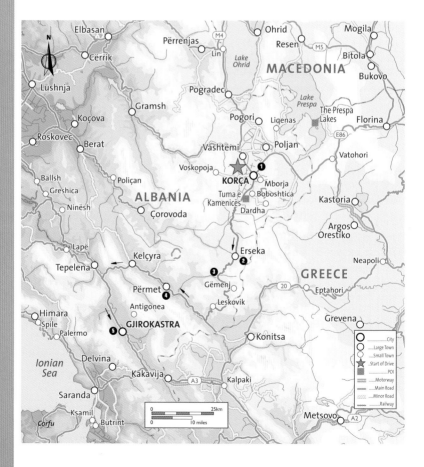

For those looking for something more bucolic, the region provides more than its fair share of mountain scenery, including the mountain villages of Voskopoja and Dardha, both within easy reach of Korça. To the north of Korça are the two majestic lakes of Prespa and Ohrid, the latter UNESCO-protected and the watery host to the intriguing lakeside town of Pogradec. A drive through the mountains may not be everyone's cup of tea, but for those willing to take on the perilous roads between Korça and Gjirokastra (*see pp82–3*), the sights along the way are more than worth the effort. Along the route discover Albania's highest town at Erseka and the pleasingly quiet and different Communist capital of Përmet. A worthwhile destination in itself or part of a more extensive itinerary, the region is just a few hours from Tirana, and even less from the Greek city of Thessaloniki.

Driving in the mountains can be testing

Korça

Set on a high plateau between the mountain ranges of southeast Albania, Korça (pronounced 'korcha') is the most important city in the region and, like Shkodra in the north, is respected throughout the country for its cultured history, its role in the Albanian national awakening and its cuisine. There's romance in the air too: the city is renowned for having the prettiest girls and has a lively tradition of serenade singing. Although the city is so close to Greece that it's easier for the locals to go shopping in Thessaloniki than in Tirana, Korça is proudly Albanian, with a variety of excellent sights both in the city and in the surroundings that merit a stay of a day or two.

Inhabited since neolithic times, Korça only blossomed after nearby Voskopoja, a major centre for Byzantine culture and art, was overrun and destroyed in the 18th century. Korça quickly developed into the regional trading centre, with a busy bazaar. The city centre consists of a few boulevards surrounded by quiet and quaint residential streets. Buses drop passengers off near the Grand Hotel on the main square, from where it's a short walk along Blvd Shën Gjergji to the landmark Orthodox church that's positioned between the modern and old town, and is a useful point of reference. Korça's oldest quarter can be found immediately behind the cathedral, where pretty cobblestoned streets wind up the slope, hiding several of the town's museums. The old bazaar area and mosque can be found just west of the main square. Blvd Republika, lined with cafés and pizzerias, leads north from the cathedral towards the city park and is closed for traffic in the evenings for the daily *xhiro*.

Tourist information

A local travel agent doubles as the tourist information centre. If contacted in advance, the English-speaking staff can help make sure the museums you wish to visit are open when you arrive and can arrange guided tours in the city and beyond.
Gulliver OK. Blvd Gjergj Kastrioti. Tel: (082) 436 97 & 068 227 0470.

Korça's Orthodox cathedral

Email: zrt_korca@yahoo.com. www.gulliver-ok.com

Bazaar

Once one of the Balkans' most important bazaars, the old warehouse buildings in Korça's old market area are rapidly deteriorating. It's still a busy daily market area with stands full of clothes, second-hand shoes, kitchen appliances, fruit, vegetables and more. Several crafts shops still function also, offering tailoring services, making tin pipes, shoes, jewellery or hats. Near the entrance of the market, the elegant **Han Elbasan** is a traditional Ottoman-era inn that was opened 200 years ago and incredibly is still in use as a hotel today. The wooden building has a courtyard with rooms where traders would leave their horses and goods for the night while they retired in the simple rooms that lined the balcony above. On the southern edge of the bazaar area, the **Xhamia e Mirahorit** (*Rruga Bajram Curri; free admission*) is Albania's oldest mosque, dating from 1494. Although it no longer has a minaret, the structure is impressive enough to have survived centuries of earthquakes and upheaval.

Birra Korça Brewery

Founded by Italians in the 1920s, an Albanian investor has recently revived the local Birra Korça brewery, using modern Czech technology and ingredients imported from Western Europe to make Albania's best Pilsner-type beers, in a light and dark variety.

Inside the Han Elbasan inn

The brew is increasingly available throughout Albania and is certainly worth trying. The old brick-built factory has been strikingly renovated and offers free tours of the premises to tourists who call in advance to book a time. After your tour, sample the brews yourself at the adjacent beer garden.
Blvd Fan S Noli 1.
Tel: (082) 429 65.
Email: info@birrakorca.com.al.
www.birrakorca.com.
Open: by appointment only.
Free admission.

Katedralja Ngallja e Krishtit (Resurrection of Christ Cathedral)
Albania's biggest Orthodox church was built a few years ago after the original cathedral was destroyed during the atheism campaign of the 1960s. The modern structure has a striking exterior, with plenty of pink paint and a tiled dome, and a light and airy interior. Visit during Mass to enjoy the characteristic choir singing.
Blvd Shën Gjergji. Open: daily.

Kisha e Mborjes (Mborja Church)
An unmissable sight for lovers of Byzantine art, the tiny 14th-century Risto ('Resurrection') church in Mborja, a village near Korça, is famed for its evocative frescoes. The church entrance shows the Day of Judgement, with the faithful entering the gates of heaven while the sinners are tortured in various imaginative ways before being sent to hell, represented by a fire-breathing dragon. Inside the simple structure, other frescoes depict saints and biblical scenes. Mborja village lies beyond the beer brewery on the eastern city limits, and can be reached by taxi or even on foot from Korça. If you find the church locked, ask for the key at the village shop.
Mborja village. Open: daily on request.

The Risto church in Mborja

Mësonjëtorja e Parë Shqipe (First Albanian School)

An elegant building surrounded by a small garden, the First Albanian School represents a very important milestone for the Albanian national awakening, and also testifies to Korça's advanced level of development. Opened in 1887 as a mixed school, it now houses the **Muzeu i Arsimit (Museum of Education)**, which is worth a visit if you have a guide to explain the exhibits and tell more about the history of the Albanian alphabet, which was only established in 1908.

Blvd Shën Gjergji.
Tel: 069 246 1792.
Open: Mon–Fri 8am–3pm, Sat & Sun by appointment. Admission charge.

Muzeu Kombëtar i Artit Mesjetar (Medieval Art Museum)

If there's time for one museum in Korça, this should be it. Housed in a former church in the old part of town, it holds Albania's best collection of icons and religious art. Two hundred of the best icons are on display, many of them made in the 17th century by artists in Voskopoja, though the oldest date back to the 14th century. Several works by Onufri (*see pp49–50*) stand out for their amazing use of colour. Contact the tourist office in advance to check if the museum is open and an English-speaking staff member is present.

Rruga Kryengritja e Qershot.
Open: Mon–Fri 8am–3pm, Sat & Sun by appointment. Admission charge.

Voskopoja

Voskopoja is a village in the green hills 20km (12 miles) west of Korça that amazingly was once the largest city of the Balkans and an important centre of Orthodox art. It is easily reached from Korça: there are buses in the morning but it's best to arrange your own transport. Before it was ruined by Ottoman campaigns in the late 18th century, Voskopoja was a bustling trading centre with over 30,000 inhabitants. The town had wide paved streets, dozens of churches and many resident writers, icon painters and other artists who helped spread the Orthodox faith. Now it's a village again, with farmhouses set between a handful of remaining churches, and the original cobbled streets still remaining as a testimony to a long-lost city.

The **Kisha e Shën Kolle (St Nicholas Church)** from 1721 is the only one currently open for visitors. It features a wonderful frescoed gallery outside and a dark interior with delicate frescoes on the walls; the icons have been moved to the Medieval Art Museum in Korça. If it's closed, ask around and someone with the key should arrive soon. If you're lucky, you may be able to track down the person holding the key to the **Kisha e Shën Thanasi (St Thanas Church)**, on the hillside to the east and also boasting well-preserved frescoes inside. The low building suffered war damage but enjoys a wonderful location amid fields of wild flowers, with good views all around. If you have time, drive or walk up to the **Manastiri i Shën Prodhamit (St Prodhami Monastery)**, hidden in the forest just east of Voskopoja, just beyond the Akademia Hotel (*see p153*). Ask the guard to let you inside the charming early 17th-century brick church in the small courtyard of the complex, where you can admire and enjoy the architecture, the iconostasis and the intense peace.

St Thanas Church in Voskopoja

A partisan statue beside Lake Ohrid

Pogradec and Liqeni i Ohrit (Lake Ohrid)

Possibly the oldest lake in Europe and the deepest lake in the Balkans, the UNESCO-protected Lake Ohrid covers an area of 358sq km (138sq miles), boasts a unique aquatic ecosystem featuring over 200 native species, is a winter habitat for a number of rare birds including the Dalmatian pelican, eastern imperial eagle, ferruginous duck and spotted eagle, and shares its waters with both Albania and neighbouring Macedonia (FYROM) to the east. Also a popular place to fish, the lake contains 17 unique species, among them the famous Ohrid trout and eight other edible varieties. The Albanian side of the lake is sprinkled with small restaurants and hotels, all of them providing opportunities to enjoy the manifold pleasures of the lake including fishing trips and the chance to simply enjoy the water on a small boat. Towards the northern end is the small lakeside village of Lin, famous for its ruined Byzantine church complete with original mosaics.

Pogradec, the largest town on the Albanian side of the lake, offers the best urban options including a couple of decent lakeside hotels and an average restaurant. Regular buses arrive in the centre from as far away as Athens and the much more local Elbasan, less than two hours away by minibus. Pogradec features a charming park by the lake, **Parku i Qytetit**, complete with old men playing dominoes and boats for hire in the summer. The only sight of particular interest is the partisan cemetery and monument on the road out of town towards Korça.

Tourist information

Pogradec's excellent informal tourist information centre, the **Internet Center**, is close to the Royal hotel and, as the name suggests, has Internet connections too.

Internet Center. Rruga Reshit Çollaku, Pall 23, Pogradec. Tel: (083) 260 80. Open: daily 9am–10pm.

The Prespa Lakes

An area of stunning natural beauty, the Prespa region holds two large lakes that are simply too beautiful to be in just one country, or even two. Prespa e Madhe (Large Prespa) is shared between Albania, Macedonia and Greece, with the Prespa e Vogël (Small Prespa) immediately to the south straddling the border with Greece. The wetlands and barren mountainous terrain surrounding the lakes are rich in wildlife, including the largest colony of Dalmatian pelicans anywhere, and there are some wonderful medieval sights to boot. The area is best visited on a guided day trip from Korça, as there are no signposts nor many English speakers. There are several simple guesthouses and a handful of restaurants serving fresh fish and local food.

The main lake is 50m (164ft) deep with rocky shores and some sandy beaches, crystal-clear waters with visibility down to 20m (66ft), and drains into Lake Ohrid through underground rivers.

The small fishing village of Liqenas on the lakeside is a good place to start exploring. Rent a boat to visit uninhabited **Maligrad Island**, a great lump of rock sticking out of the water. The 14th-century **Kisha e Shën Meri (St Mary's Church)** is situated high up in a cave on the island and is reached by clambering up steep and shaky wooden ladders, a climb rewarded by the sight of precious Byzantine murals and the views back across the lake. Reached by boat from Gorica e Madhe village, the steep cliffs of the peninsula near the Macedonian border hide another rock church, the Shën Maria (St Maria), as well as several monastic cells, some perched as high as 40m (130ft) above the lake. Several cells have impressive 15th-century frescoes.

SHEPHERDS

Drive your car to the top of the tallest mountain you can find in the most remote part of Albania, switch off the engine and get out. Far from being away from it all as you suspected, not only will you almost certainly see a concrete bunker or two (*see p13*), you'll probably also hear the clattering and tinkling of bells. Peer over the edge into the abyss and perched somewhere down there on a rock, probably dressed in ill-fitting suit and baseball cap, will be a man and his sheep. The lifeline for thousands of otherwise impoverished country folk and carrying on an age-old tradition, shepherding in Albania provides both dairy products and meat in a land where unemployment is widespread and state financial support remains a far-off dream.

Drive: Korça to Gjirokastra

The spectacular drive from Korça to Gjirokastra may look easy on the map, but don't let Albanian cartography get the better of you. Taking in part of the Gramoz mountain range, the only road connecting the two towns feels like little more than a donkey track in places, though a 4WD car is not necessary. This trip is not for the faint-hearted!

The journey is just 195 km (121 miles) but allow a minimum of five hours. See p74 for route.

Start in Korça. Take the main road south out of town.

1 Korça to Erseka

The first part of the journey to Erseka introduces the driver to the rigours of mountain driving in Albania, climbing up gradually for about 30km (19 miles) and taking up to an hour. After 10km (6 miles), stop off at the **Tuma e Kamenicës (Tumulus of Kamenica)** archaeological site, a wonderful, newly excavated prehistoric burial mound

Stunning scenery along the route

with a museum and guided tours in English (*tel: 069 268 7009; www.kamenicatumulus.org; open: May–Sept 9am–7pm, Oct–Apr 8am–4pm; closed: Mon; admission charge*).

2 Erseka

At 900m (2,950ft) above sea level, Erseka is the highest town in Albania. It boasts a proud and patriotic mountain people and a somewhat alpine feel. Find the central square and enjoy a break in one of the cafés. Nearby is the local **Historical and Ethnographic Museum** featuring some fine examples of local arts and crafts (*open: erratic hours; admission charge*). Relax here before launching into the fun part of the journey.

Slowly descend back towards sea level on one of the wiggliest and most frightening roads in Albania.

3 Erseka to Gëmenj

One minute you are plunged into darkness as you plough through a thick pine forest, the next minute turning endless hairpins as the road clings perilously to the edge of the mountain. At the tiny settlement of Gëmenj is **Vila Jorgo** (*tel: 069 240 9641*), offering a further refreshment stop, small zoo and even a bed for the night if you need it. *Head north once you're off the mountains.*

4 Përmet

The highly recommended town of Përmet is almost affluent-looking. Famous for its roses and the unofficial Communist capital of Albania, Përmet features a lovely central square, named after the national hero and Albanian diplomat Abdyl Frashëri (1839–92), and the average Orthodox St Michael's Church up on the hill. The town's main theme, however, is given away by the huge Socialist-Realist statue of a partisan on the western edge of the square, the work of the Albanian sculptor and patron of the arts Odhisë Paskali (1903–85), who was also responsible for the large Skanderbeg statue in Tirana. Burned to the ground several times during World War II, Përmet played a significant political role in Albania: it was here in 1944 that the so-called Congress of Përmet created the provisional government, outlawed any fascist activity in Albania, banned King Zog from the country and essentially paved the way for the Hoxha regime. Highly recommended for visitors looking for the authentic Communist experience, Përmet has the

Partisan monument in Përmet

decent Përmeti Hotel in the square (*see p152*), impressive mountain vistas and is the obvious place to break the journey.

Keep heading north through the mountain valleys with the Vjosa River on your left for a further 30km (19 miles) or so until you cross a small bridge over the Drinos River and reach the main road. Take a right for a trip to Tepelena (see p106) or go left towards Gjirokastra, following the main road south for a further 25km (15 miles). En route, you might like to take one of the bridges on the left back over the river and up the mountainside for a spectacular view.

5 Gjirokastra

Your final destination will not disappoint. As a World Heritage Site of incredible beauty, Gjirokastra will enthrall you (*see pp104–6*).

Southern Albania

If you had one choice of where you could base yourself when planning a few days in Albania, you could do much worse than southern Albania. Stretching some 170km (106 miles) of fabulous coastline from the fiercely patriotic northern port of Vlora all the way down to the country's most impressive archaeological site at Butrint, and not forgetting the many sights and sensations to be discovered to the land-locked east, southern Albania really has got everything a holiday destination is supposed to offer.

Independence monument in Vlora

If all you want from your holiday are a few square metres of white sand next to the sea on which to soak up the sun, the range of beaches along the Albanian Riviera are full of temptation, whether the temptation comes in the form of the peaceful coves around Ksamil or the more upbeat beaches around the larger towns. If beaches aren't your thing, or if you need more than the pleasures of a bottle of suntan oil, satisfy an architectural itch or two among the ruins of Butrint or the Ottoman old bazaar of Gjirokastra. Like its neighbouring region to the east, southern Albania's complicated history makes the drawing of clear ethnic lines folly. This is the Balkans, don't forget, and here in southern Albania you're as likely to hear Greek spoken in many towns as you are

the state tongue. Whatever language the people are speaking, expect everyone to welcome you with a strange mix of pleasure and curiosity, the kind usually found in the more provincial parts of China rather than in a country less than 100km (62 miles) from Italy.

Last but by no means least, Albania's location next to the sea guarantees an endless stream of seafood to keep the brain alert and the palate dancing.

VLORA AND THE BAY
Vlora

The second-largest port in Albania, the big and generally unattractive city of Vlora offers visitors two main reasons for stopping by. First, it's got some great beaches on either side of the bay, and second, it's the spiritual home of

The Independence Museum building once housed the Albanian government

Albanian independence. Reachable by ferry from the Italian port of Brindisi and by hydrofoil shuttling between Corfu, Saranda and Himara, Vlora can also be reached via buses from Athens, Tirana, Saranda and scores of other Albanian destinations. Boats arrive in the main harbour, close to the main sights. All buses terminate and leave from the area in front of Xamia e Muradies (Muradi Mosque, *see opposite*).

Muzeu Etnografik (Ethnographic Museum)

This intriguing museum, hidden away in what looks like a car park opposite the Muzeu Historik (Historical Museum), charts the history of the local independence movement as well as highlighting the life and culture of the people of the region. A visual feast indeed, like most museums in Albania, the lack of any information in English can be somewhat off-putting.
Tel: (033) 235 14. Open: Tue–Fri 8am–2pm & 5–8pm, Sat & Sun 9am–noon. Closed: Mon. Admission charge.

Muzeu Historik (Historical Museum)

Not always open when it says it is, the city's Historical Museum, immediately northeast of Sheshi i Flamurit (Flag Square) in the house on the corner, contains a fine collection of artefacts charting the history of the town and region. The museum also has a good selection of related literature for sale. Bang hard on the door if it's locked.
Tel: (033) 235 34. Open: Tue–Sun 8am–2pm. Closed: Mon. Admission charge.

Muzeu i Pavarësisë (Independence Museum)

A former quarantine hospital and the site of the first Albanian government in 1912, this building next to the port features re-creations of how the building looked before World War I, among other independence-related paraphernalia. *Tel: (033) 294 19. Open: Tue–Sun 8am–1pm & 5–8pm. Closed: Mon. Admission charge.*

Sheshi i Flamurit (Flag Square)

A simple concrete space brightened up with the Socialist-Realist centrepiece, the **Monumenti i Pavarësisë (Independence Monument)**. It was on this spot that the Albanian flag was first raised over an independent nation on 28 November 1912.

Xhamia e Muradies (Muradi Mosque)

Built some time during the middle of the 16th century, this lovely mosque features a repeating white stone and red brick pattern. The roof, with its wavy red tiles, resembles that of an Orthodox church.

The Bay

Situated in the middle of Vlora Bay, the city is a good base for a couple of excursions. As well as several fine beaches (*see pp88–90*), 10km (6 miles) south of the city is the 6th-century BC site of Orikum. Beyond this is the **Kepi i Gjuhëzës (Karaburun Peninsula)**, a desolate spit of land worth a few hours' exploration. The peninsula is very hilly, with little in the way of access to any of the beaches on it. Be sure to let somebody know where you're going if you do decide to explore the area in detail.

To the north of the city at the southern end of the Narta Lagoon there's a fine 14th-century Byzantine church, which could possibly be included in a northern excursion taking in Apollonia (*see pp46–7*) and Ardenica (*see p55*) as well.

Muradi Mosque

Beaches

Albania's beaches are among the most beautiful in Europe and play an important role in the current development of tourism. Still untouched by massive development projects, the Albanian coastline resembles the world as it was before the creeping claws of Capitalism transformed the rest of the Mediterranean, offering visitors the perfect blend of classic stretches of white sand punctuated with the occasional utopian bay or cove. Don't take your time booking your holiday, however – the bulldozers are already warming up, and much of the coastline, especially along several stretches of the glorious Albanian Riviera, are already earmarked for some truly vulgar resorts.

Albania basically has two types of coastal areas: the long sandy beaches backed by flat lowland to the north of Vlora, and to the south the Riviera, where the mountains drop steeply to the sea. There are also some beaches near Pogradec along Lake Ohrid. In case you're wondering, Albania has only a handful of small islands. Some are near Ksamil in the south, and Sazan Island near Vlora is used by the military and is closed to visitors.

While some beach areas have been spoiled by unchecked and often illegal construction, many of Albania's beaches are still completely virgin and it's not difficult to find a quiet spot. The beaches near the main towns have chair and parasol rental and are lined with restaurants and hotels, while on more isolated beaches you may find some taverns but you'll have to bring everything else yourself. Facilities like showers, swimming pools, children's playgrounds and lifeguards are mainly absent, or only provided by more upmarket hotels. This makes choosing a good hotel important when planning a beach holiday in Albania.

Beautiful turquoise seas north of Borsh

Some parts of the coast, like here at Dhermi, are completely undeveloped (for now)

Popular beaches along the coast of northern Albania include Velipoja near Shkodra, Shëngjin near Lezha and the long beach at Durrës and Golem. All of these are very crowded during summer months. South of Vlora, sandy coves and pebble bays line the coast all the way to the Greek border, with great beaches at Dhërmi, Himara, Qeparo and Borsh. With a good map, private transport and persistence, you'll find lovely quiet beaches elsewhere, for instance amid the lagoons at Ishull-Lezha, at Seman west of Fier and Apollonia and, for the truly adventurous looking for a desert island experience, around the wild Karaburun Peninsula to the west of Vlora.

Environmental problems bedevil many of Albania's beaches. The presence of untreated sewage makes it wise to avoid swimming in the direct proximity of harbours and large towns and cities including Durrës, Vlora, Saranda and Pogradec. Additionally, there's often rubbish on the beach or in the water as trash gets washed up or people litter. Due to lack of political will, Albania remains the last country with a coastline in Europe that still has no Blue Flag-rated beaches, though as the authorities are increasingly put to shame over this, things may change soon.

Assuming you don't mind a certain lack of polished service and amenities, taking a beach holiday along Albania's Adriatic and Ionian coastline can't come recommended enough.

THE ALBANIAN RIVIERA

Reachable via one of the most perilous, winding, narrow and still in several places astonishingly bumpy roads in Europe, the Albanian Riviera consists of countless beaches scattered down the 130km (81-mile) stretch of Adriatic and Ionian coastline from Vlora in the north to Saranda and the Greek border beyond. The Riviera offers a relatively unspoiled adventure for anyone who enjoys beach culture, whether that involves the art of lying on a lounger and slowly changing colour or dashing about the turquoise-blue waves on windsurf boards. The fact that the coastline is also covered in hotels and places to eat, all of them still exceedingly good value for money compared to even such places as Croatia and the emerging resorts along the Montenegrin coast, means that a beach holiday along the Riviera can't be too highly recommended. There really are too many good beaches to mention, but among the great and the good, the best beaches include the well-equipped small cove at Spile, complete with pink and blue painted bunkers, pedalo hire and a decent restaurant, the long pebble beach at Borsh, offering even more bunkers and a night-club, the spectacular beach at Dhërmi, the magnificent Piqeras and, last but not least, the little island paradise south of Saranda at Ksamil.

However, although primarily a destination for beach holidays, the Riviera also offers a few other sights of interest along the way, and can be enjoyed with the help of a car over a period of a few leisurely days of driving. Punctuated with charming little villages, small fishing ports, jaw-droppingly astounding scenery of mountains covered in olive and citrus trees as well as a couple of destinations worthy of more than a quick refreshment break, the Albanian Riviera is not to be missed.

The Llogora Pass

Separating Vlora and the start of the main stretch of the Albanian Riviera to the south, the spectacular Llogora Pass will both inspire you and test your

A ferry leaving Saranda for Corfu

The Llogora Pass is extremely steep in places, providing great views of the coast

vehicle like it's never been tested before. The pass road climbs very steeply to 1,027m (3,369ft) above sea level, offering stunning views of the Adriatic and wildlife in abundance. Popular with naturalists who come to spot deer, wild boar, the occasional wolf and several species of birds including owls, eagles and woodpeckers, the Llogora Pass has little in the way of amenities save a few restaurants and hotels just north of the top, all famous for their delicious spit-roast lamb washed down with several glasses of the local firewater. As the seawater starts to boil at the height of the summer season, the cool altitude provides welcome relief and is worth thinking about as a base away from the human lobsters frying

away on the beaches far below. A highly recommended option is the **Fshati Turistik (Tourist Village,** *see p155*), which as well as providing superb accommodation in wooden chalets also has plenty of things to keep you occupied, including walking trails and, for the more adventurous, supervised rock-climbing expeditions and even paragliding. Although horrendously steep and winding, the road over the pass is now fully paved and has also been widened. The climb down from the top in the direction of Saranda takes you through the tiny settlement of Palasa, where Julius Caesar and seven full legions landed in 49 BC on their way to fight a battle at Kajava Crag in the north.

Northern Riviera

The Northern Riviera starts more or less in the port city of Vlora and is covered in more detail under 'Vlora and the bay' (*see pp85–7*). If you're planning to drive the route from north to south, you could consider taking in Orikum and the Karaburun Peninsula (*see p87*) on the way. Between these first destinations, the road south of the tunnel marking the edge of the city goes past the Paradise Beach hotel (*see p157*) and follows the coast for several kilometres, offering a few beaches and little more before snaking inland at Orikum and on over the Llogora Pass.

The spectacular drive that climbs up and over the Llogora Pass (*see pp90–91*) offers no access to the coast, but the views of the sea are some of the best in the country. Stopping for a meal in one of the restaurants at the top is literally one of the highlights of the trip. Coming down the road and off the pass takes you through the small village of Palasa (*see p91*) and on to **Dhërmi**, a lovely little settlement which, as well as boasting an idyllic white sandy beach with crystal-clear water and plenty of amenities, also offers a few pleasant walks in among citrus groves and olive trees. The beach is reached via a small road on top of the hill close to the Dorian Hotel (*see p153*). Just south of Dhërmi on the main road is the small Panorama café-bar that only sells drinks, but has a spectacular terrace overlooking the beach far down below. Dhërmi was a particular favourite of Edward Lear (*see p97*), who visited in 1844, both writing about and painting the surrounding region.

The final few kilometres between Dhërmi and the town of Himara provide several options for drivers. The main road follows the coast a little inland and offers spectacular scenery

Driving through the northern part of the Albanian Riviera

Himara's stunning location

but little else. Alternatively, you could risk getting hopelessly lost on one or other of the two tiny tracks that loop off the main road down to a couple of quiet beaches and coves. During the summer, the area gears up a little to the local tourist trade, and small bars open along the waterfront, but there's not much else to be found. If you're looking for a relaxing break that takes in both the very best of unspoiled beaches and opportunities to walk in the surrounding hilly countryside, the area between Dhërmi and Himara is well worth considering, although you'll have to choose between staying in one of the two towns as there's nothing else on offer.

Himara itself is a lovely town nestled in a bay and surrounded by high mountains. As you enter the town from the north, up on the hill to the right is the castle. The spot is believed to have been inhabited for over 3,000 years. The current structure, which is in fairly terrible condition, has Byzantine and Ottoman elements, reflecting both the age and strategic importance of the town. There are beaches on either side of the centre, some sand and some pebble. The new Rapo's Resort Hotel (*see p155*), on the southern edge of Himara and coming with its own private beach, is a good place to spend the night. The town centre itself is small, with one little road next to the bus station that leads directly onto the beach. The road has several outdoor cafés, and there's even a small private tourist information centre, which at the time of writing had nothing in English, although plans are afoot to publish information for English-speaking visitors during 2009.

Southern Riviera

One of the loveliest parts of Albania, the spectacular Southern Riviera between Himara and the small seaside town of Ksamil just south of Saranda offers an extraordinary number of treats, from jagged mountains diving into the clear blue sea to restaurants in the middle of nowhere serving fish caught that morning and a much-welcome new enterprise catering to the more adventurous traveller. Following on from the journey south along the Northern Riviera, this short section features the best and most diverse things to see and do in the region, including a couple of options inland away from the coast.

The few kilometres of winding coastal road between Himara and the

ALI PASHA TEPELENA

Born near Tepelena during the height of Ottoman supremacy in the Balkans, Ali Pasha Tepelena (1741–1822) emerged as the leading ruler of the southern half of Albania and what is now northwestern Greece. Through a combination of shrewd diplomacy and good old-fashioned violence, Ali Pasha Tepelena played the part of a local empire builder, leaving his architectural signatures all over the region. Almost every town in southern Albania can claim to have something built by him, and there's more than one castle said to have been built by him dotted along the coast, including the one at Palermo, just south of Himara. To date no Ali Pasha Tepelena tours exist. As Albania, the only country in the Balkans without any chip on its shoulder about the Ottoman period, develops, it's only a matter of time before one emerges.

tiny port at Palermo feature some truly beautiful landscape and the recommended and popular beach at Spile (*see p90*). Look for a track on a right-hand bend that leads to a modern building by the sea. In a little bay with plenty of amenities, you can spend a very relaxing day here.

With the exception of the scenery, there's little else of note heading south until you reach **Palermo**. Just before Palermo as you round the bend to the left you'll see on your right the old Communist-era, Soviet-funded submarine base complete with bombproof housing inside the cliff face. The people who own Tirana's Rogner Hotel are allegedly planning to convert the base into a holiday resort. Club Med is also planning to develop this stretch of coastline. Get there and enjoy it before it's too late. Palermo is a must-see destination, worthy of a stop of at least two hours. The Porto Palermo restaurant on the left-hand side of the road serves freshly caught cod from the little fishing harbour opposite, plus handmade fries and excellent salads. The castle here was another Ali Pasha Castle, built by the frenetic and industrious Ali Pasha Tepelena (*see box*) at the start of the 19th century. The triangular building with three towers is worth poking around, although there are no organised tours.

The beach at **Borsh** (*see p90*) a little further along can be reached by turning right immediately after the

A winding coastal road on the Southern Riviera

petrol station and following the concrete track along past the bunkers. A few kilometres further south is **Piqeras**, a small but popular beach resort complete with its own pier and accommodation, including a few beds in several converted bunkers nearby. The resort has a clean sandy beach as well as restaurants and loud bars during the summer season.

Heading inland again on the final few kilometres towards Saranda is the village of **Shën Vasil**. In the corner of the main square you'll see the Studio

THE *XHIRO*

From the Italian *giro* ('tour' or 'circuit') and pronounced the same way, the *xhiro* sees every town in Albania coming out to parade at 6pm sharp, daily. Most spectacular on a summer evening, the *xhiro* is part mating ritual, part catwalk and part social event and involves everyone from babies in prams to old men and women. Simple in the extreme, the idea is to walk endlessly up and down a street until you get bored or bump into somebody and go off and do something else. All *xhiro* streets have at least one café for spectators to complete the effect, and in many places the police close off streets for traffic to allow for safe strolling.

The beach at Borsh, complete with concrete bunkers

Looking down the valley from Shën Vasil

Mex restaurant. A good spot for a bite to eat, on closer inspection Studio Mex is in actual fact the nerve centre of an extraordinary one-man operation. The genial Ernesto who runs the place spent several years in Germany and has brought his Western talents home with the intention of making the local area a tourist paradise. The upstairs of the restaurant has a few self-catering apartments and a top-floor penthouse room for lovers complete with a round bed and mirrors on the ceiling. Ernesto can also organise everything from 4WD hire and accommodation to parties on the beach and paragliding.

Studio Mex. Tel: 069 280 8068.
www.holidaysinalbania.de

EDWARD LEAR

More famous in his homeland for his limericks and nonsense literature, Englishman Edward Lear (1812–88) is known throughout Albania not only as a painter, but as a painter who visited and painted the country extensively. In his mid-20s Lear left England and travelled for the rest of his life, visiting Albania in his late 30s and through his 40s, where he drew, painted and wrote copiously about the strange sights and sensations the country had to offer under Ottoman rule. He was particularly fond of the southern half of the country, and the art gallery in Berat (*see p50*), a town that furnished Lear with the inspiration for countless drawings and paintings, is even named after him. Those interested in knowing more should get hold of a copy of the excellent book *Edward Lear in the Levant: Travels in Albania, Greece and Turkey in Europe, 1848–49*, published by John Murray (1988).

SARANDA

One of the sunniest places in Europe, Saranda is a fabulous destination for those looking for an urban base from which to make forays to some of the best and most diverse sights in Albania. Inside a horseshoe bay, and barely 10km (6 miles) from Corfu, Saranda comes with its own intriguing Albanian and Greek cultures. The town attracts some of the country's better-off citizens, who like nothing more than to stroll along the traffic-free promenade every evening for their *xhiro* (*see p96*). Within easy driving distance of Butrint as well as a few quiet beaches along the coast in either direction, Saranda is well worth staying in for a night or two.

Saranda is served by buses from inside Albania as well as from Greece, via the border crossing at Qafëbota.

Buses arrive and depart five minutes north of the waterfront, close to the Lindi Hotel. Arriving in Saranda by car is possible along a choice of perilously narrow roads including the Greek border in the south. Regular ferries and hydrofoils ply the short, watery trip between Saranda and Corfu and arrive at the small terminal to the west of the harbour. The hydrofoil doesn't run during the winter.

In town

Just north of the harbour is what's left of the town's synagogue. Built in around the 6th century, the synagogue ended its days as a Christian church before being destroyed. A small hut, with erratic opening times, has more information. Visible from the waterfront, the 1993 Orthodox church

The remains of the synagogue at Saranda

has some fine modern golden
chandeliers and icons inside.

Muzeu i Arsimit (Heritage Museum)

Inside the old Ottoman customs
building on the waterfront in the
middle of town, this museum records
the major events of the town's history
using a small collection of artefacts, all
labelled in Albanian only.
Open: 8am–6pm. Admission charge.

Out of town

Ksamil

Twenty minutes south of Saranda is
this popular resort, a typically chaotic
Albanian town with dirt roads and half-
built houses, but the effort of finding the
beach is worth it. Its charming little bay
has four wooded islands with white
sandy beaches. During the summer,
locals cook and sell fresh seafood on the
islands, which can be reached by boats
hired from people along the main beach
or, for the more adventurous, by
swimming from island to island. Ksamil
beach itself has a few bars and
restaurants plus accommodation
options (*see p155*).

Syri i Kalter (Blue Eye)

About 25km (15 miles) east of Saranda
on the southernmost of the two roads
that take you to Gjirokastra is Syri i
Kalter. The small pool at the end of a
lake is connected to a deep underground
spring that pours a constant stream of
water to the surface. The combination
of the depth of the hole, the clarity of

The Blue Eye

the water and the quality of the light
turns the pool into what appears to be
a large blue eye, complete with a black
eyeball in the middle. The site includes
a restaurant and cabins to stay in
(*see p156*).

Look for the Syri i Kalter sign from
the main road, follow the track to the
left and round the edge of the reservoir
and keep going until you pass through
two white posts. It's another minute or
two from here. To avoid confusion, be
aware that Syri i Kalter is the name
given to several other similar sights
around the country.

The bathhouse at Butrint World Heritage Site

BUTRINT

Situated about 14km (9 miles) south of Saranda on the main road along the coast, the **Parku Kombëtar i Butrintit (Butrint National Park)** covers an area of 25ha (62 acres) and includes a large lake, wetlands and a host of other natural sights. The park draws nature-lovers of all persuasions for its wealth of wildlife including several rare species of birds and plants, but the unquestionable highlight of the area is the ancient archaeological site of Butrint, after which the park was named. Butrint was founded by the Greek-speaking Chaonians, and evidence suggests that a settlement has been on this site since around the 9th century BC. Absorbed into the Roman Empire in 228 BC when it was known as Bouthroton, Butrint grew into a substantial colony complete with aqueduct, bathhouse, amphitheatre and

even a cathedral, much of which can still be seen today. Julius Caesar famously used Butrint as a base for military provisions during the 1st century BC. It was abandoned some time around the 16th century.

Excavations on Butrint began in 1928, led by the Italian archaeologist Luigi Ugolini (1895–1936), working under the direct instructions of Mussolini. Butrint became a UNESCO World Heritage Site in 1992. The national park was set up in 2000. In this blissful haven of eucalyptus trees and crumbling buildings, a full tour of the site can take all day. Most people, however, will be satisfied with a leisurely walk around the marked trail, which takes somewhere in the region of two hours. Take a bottle or two of drinking water if visiting during the summer.

Regular buses leave the centre of Saranda close to the Lindi Hotel, are extremely cheap and can take up to an hour to make the journey. A taxi will cost you at least 50 times more, not including what you'll need to pay to get the driver to wait before taking you back again. The drive down is fairly unremarkable although there are a couple of beaches with facilities along the way, including the beach and islands at Ksamil (*see p99*). The road was built in 1959 in order to drive Nikita Khrushchev to the area during a state visit. The famously uncultured Russian leader was unimpressed, suggesting it would make a good submarine base.

The entrance to the site is at the end of the road from Saranda, next to the cable ferry. Follow the signs in an anti-clockwise direction. The following information explains a little about the main things to see but is by no means comprehensive. Tourist information is in the small wooden shed at the entrance to the site, where you can buy guides and maps for the tour.

Amphitheatre

Dating from around the 3rd century BC, the remarkably well-preserved amphitheatre is the first main sight on the trail. Built to seat up to 3,000 people, it still hosts events.

Baptistery

The 6th-century baptistery is famous for being one of the largest in Eastern Europe. As the name implies, this was where people were brought to be converted to Christianity. The font is still intact; the water in it was heated courtesy of the classic Roman hypocaust system, of which much remains. The floor retains many of its original mosaics but is covered for protection.

Basilica

Featuring architectural details from the 6th century or earlier, the basilica is beautifully preserved and worth a good look around.

Museum and acropolis

Not actually on the main walk, the site of the former acropolis is now given over to the museum, which contains many of the artefacts found during excavation work on the site.

The amphitheatre

Walk: Butrint Bay Trail

To make a day out of a trip to Butrint, consider combining a walk around the archaeological site with this one, just across the water. The area around the archaeological site features many more fabulous architectural and archaeological ruins, including Roman cemeteries, an aqueduct, and castles from the times of both the Venetian and Ottoman occupations. Although it doesn't cover any major archaeological sites due to the sheer size of the area, the walk does give you an idea of what else there is.

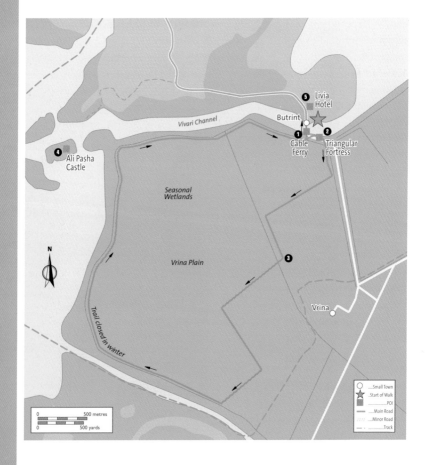

Note that this walk isn't possible during the winter, when much of the land is entirely under water. Download the brochure with detailed maps and longer walks in the park at the excellent website www.butrint.org

The Butrint Bay Trail is reached by ferry and is about 6km (4 miles) in total, covering a completely flat area of land, making it attractive to people of all ages. Allow one or two hours.

Start at the small ferry directly outside the main Butrint site.

1 Cable ferry

Although it doesn't look like it, the road from Saranda to Butrint is a fairly major one by Albanian standards. Regardless of the fact that it's the only coastal road that links directly with Greece, there remains much work to be done to get the road in order, including at the point here where it crosses the water. To get to the other side, jump on the thing that looks like a huge door connected to the land at either end by a wire. This is the car ferry. There is a small charge for foot passengers. The crossing takes about a minute.

Back on dry land, turn east along the muddy track that also serves as the main road.

2 Heading east

To your left is the Venetian Triangular Fortress, built in around 1490 by the once powerful Republic of Venice, who owned this land and Corfu at the time. Named after its unconventional shape, the fortress was used to protect the local fishing industry, one of the major industries of the region at the time.

Take the first turning on your right, just before the road turns in the same direction, and head south. Follow the path round to the right, towards the centre of the plain.

3 Vrina and beyond

This area is a haven for much wildlife, including 26 endangered species, among them marginated tortoises (Europe's largest), wolves and white-tailed eagles.

Keep the small village of Vrina on your left and follow the zigzagging path up to the little river and turn right. Keep the water on your left and keep walking.

4 Ali Pasha Castle

As the track makes a sharp right after 2.5km (1 1/2 miles), on your left on an island you'll see the remains of a castle allegedly built by Ali Pasha Tepelena (*see p94*) but probably dating from the Venetian era.

Follow the track back along to the ferry and ride it over the water again. When you disembark, head up the road.

5 Livia Hotel

On your right is the Livia Hotel, the perfect place to finish off your walk with some food and drink in the garden if you're not actually staying here.

Southern Albania

GJIROKASTRA

The UNESCO-protected museum city of Gjirokastra is a masterpiece of Ottoman ingenuity. Perched perilously on the edge of a steep hill covered in unique grey houses and overlooked by a huge and impressive castle, Gjirokastra was the birthplace of two important figures in contemporary Albanian history, namely Enver Hoxha and the Booker Prize-winning author Ismail Kadare (1936–).

It's less than half an hour from the Greek border, and buses leave daily for Gjirokastra from Ioannina along a road that's one of the best in the country. There are also regular buses from Saranda plus a few from Tirana. Public transport arrives at the bus station in the new part of town, a 20-minute walk up the hill from the main sights, which are all packed closely together.

A view of Gjirokastra from the castle

Tourist information

For more extensive information about the city and surrounding region, visit the excellent little tourist information centre (*tel: (084) 670 77 & 069 237 3093; open: Tue–Sun 9am–5pm; closed: Mon*), first left up the hill after the Sopoti Hotel in the old bazaar. The friendly staff here can provide brochures and maps and organise guided tours. An initiative of the Gjirokastra Conservation and Development Organization, their website (*www.gjirokastra.org*) has more information.

Kalaja e Gjirokastrës (Gjirokastra Castle)

Looking like a huge ship stranded on top of a hill after a flood, Gjirokastra's fortified masterpiece castle probably dates from as far back as the 3rd century BC, although the current walls went up 900 years later. The castle has been enlarged and improved over the centuries, but time has taken its toll on the structure, although a few points of interest, notably the clock tower dating from the time of Ali Pasha Tepelena, still exists. The castle is also home to the Muzeu Kombëtar i Armëve (National Armaments Museum, *see opposite*), which proudly and somewhat bizarrely displays the rotting remains of a USAF reconnaissance plane shot down in 1957, found on the wall in the northeastern part of the complex. In between the clock tower and the plane is a flight of steps leading to a bar, which is nothing to write

The captured USAF plane on display at Gjirokastra Castle

home about but is considerably cooler than the outside temperature, a fact worth remembering if you're visiting during the summer. The ugly-looking spaceship thing incidentally is the main stage for the International Folk Music Festival (*see p19*), held every four years in September. The next is scheduled for 2012. Two chirpy gentlemen in purple suits and peaked caps guard the castle entrance and are there to sell you a ticket.
Tel: (084) 624 60. Open: 9am–7pm. Admission charge.

Muzeu Etnografik (Ethnographic Museum)

Not far from the Kalema Hotel just north of the centre of the old bazaar, this house is famous for being the birthplace of Enver Hoxha. This isn't actually quite the case, as the original building burned down in 1916 and wasn't rebuilt for a further 50 years. The museum is stuffed full of fascinating exhibits as well as re-creations of the rooms as they would have appeared a century ago. Take a moment to admire the wonderfully ornate, carved wooden ceilings.
Open: 9am–7pm. Admission charge.

Muzeu Kombëtar i Armëve (National Armaments Museum)

Inside the former castle prison block that also serves as the entrance (and was holding convicts up until 1971), the museum contains plenty of hardware including the aforementioned aeroplane, several old cannons and a Fiat tank from World War II. The rest of the collection includes the usual displays of uniforms and photographs, and is in Albanian only.
Gjirokastra Castle. Tel: (084) 624 60. Open: 9am–7pm. Admission charge.

Other sights

A recommended way to see the city is to get your bearings first by visiting the castle before anywhere else. Not only is the view wonderful, it's also a useful way of getting an idea of how the old bazaar (*pazari i vjetër*) below is laid out. The centre of the old bazaar, built primarily in the first half of the 19th century, features several fine examples of Ottoman social housing, much of which is in a pretty bad way. The houses of Gjirokastra are famous for their uniqueness, being slightly different in their design to other Ottoman houses in Albania. A guided

The heart of the old bazaar in Gjirokastra

tour from a local expert will help you get the most from what is a fairly simple set of modifications designed along defensive lines. One good example is the birthplace of Ismail Kadare, which features classic Gjirokastra-style architectural details and is also a place of pilgrimage for fans of the author.

Down from the old bazaar is the main square, built on an alarmingly steep slope and named after Çerçiz Topulli, a local hero who organised an uprising against the Turks in 1908 and whose statue takes pride of place on the square's southern side. At the bottom of the square is the Greek consular building, easily identified on weekday mornings by the huge line of Albanians queuing for visas.

TEPELENA AND BYLLIS

Some 30km (19 miles) north of Gjirokastra on the road to Fier and Tirana, the small town of Tepelena was once a significant and strategically important Byzantine and Ottoman settlement, to which the grand albeit crumbling fortress on the hill testifies. On the western bank of the Vjosa River, Tepelena continued to be an important Turkish town right up until the First Balkan War of 1912 and was visited over the centuries by a catalogue of illustrious figures including Lord Byron, who spent time at the court of Ali Pasha and after whom the town's main square is named. Famous today for its mineral water and little else, the town is worth a quick look. Of note are the desolate fortress and square, as well as a small bronze bust of the Albanian freedom fighter Selam Musai (1860–1920) on the road north out of town.

About halfway between Tepelena and Fier lies the archaeological site of ancient Byllis. Just a few kilometres east of the main road, this enormous site, covering some 30ha (74 acres) on top of a hill close to the Vjosa River, was founded by the Illyrians and dates from at least the 4th century BC. Occupied until just after AD 586 when it was ransacked by invading Slav tribes, much of the original settlement still exists, including parts of a cathedral, amphitheatre, several gates and some fine mosaics – though it's not as evocative as Butrint or Apollonia. The site is signposted from the main road and can be reached by car. A café and information centre are on site. *www.byllis-al.com. Open: daily 9am–5pm. Free admission.*

The Selam Musai monument north of Tepelena

Getting away from it all

In a way, all of Albania could be labelled 'off the beaten track', but even for a country with few visitors, there are some particularly lovely spots where you can truly get away from it all. Reaching the following four destinations takes time, energy and a sore back from the bumpy roads and may require some advance planning, but all of them offer a wonderful, relaxing break from the more touristy parts of the country.

Dardha

One of Albania's prettiest villages lies 20km (12 miles) south of Korça in a lush forested valley at an altitude of just over 1,300m (4,300ft), opposite the Guri i Vjeshtës ('Autumn Stone') mountain. Reached in 45 minutes from the city by taxi or daily *furgon* minibus over a gravel road, Dardha was founded in the 17th century by Christian families fleeing from Ottoman conversion efforts and currently has only about 50 inhabitants. The village consists of picturesque cobblestone lanes lined with old stone houses, most in a surprisingly good state by Albanian standards, and the Kisha e Shën Gjergjit (St George Church).

There are some modern buildings at the entrance of the village, but otherwise Dardha has a rustic and original feel to it. Dardha is famous for its fresh mountain air and for the mineral water flowing from several public wells, one named Uji e qelbur ('dirty water') for the smell of sulphur. Apart from their very frank manner of talking (nicknamed *Sepata e Dardha*, or 'Dardha axes'), the villagers are well known for their black and red traditional costumes and for the huge and delicious double-layered onion and tomato pies they bake, called *lakror*.

Accommodation is offered in a few modern hotels, but for the real

Lura Lakes

Dardha village is filled with pretty stone houses and narrow lanes

experience it's worth asking around for a traditional guesthouse, where you can expect to be pampered and fed till you burst. If you're still hungry by the time you leave, on the plain halfway between Korça and Dardha you'll pass Boboshtica, a village with several good restaurants specialising in grilled lamb dishes as well as *lakror* pie and several exotic varieties of *raki*, including mulberry. The tourist information office in Korça (*see p76*) can help with up-to-date information about Dardha accommodation and transport.

Liqenet e Lurës (Lura Lakes)

Set between high peaks 125km (77 miles) to the northeast of Tirana, the remote Parku Kombëtar i Lurës (Lura National Park) is a well-known but little-visited beauty spot, characterised by meadows full of flowers, lush forests and a dozen glacial lakes of varying size, set at altitudes between 1,200m and 1,600m (4,000ft and 5,250ft) below the Kurora e Lurës (Crown of Lura) mountain range. The four largest lakes are the Leqeni i Madh (Great Lake), Leqeni i Zi (Black Lake), Leqeni i Luleve (Lake of Flowers) and the Liqeni i Lopeve (Cow Lake). In summer, some of the lakes fill up with beautiful water lilies.

Apart from wandering around the lakes and pine forests, climbing the nearby mountains and picnicking in the fields, there's blissfully little to do. The one annoyance is the illegal logging which has taken its toll on the area and is still ongoing, even within the national park boundaries.

The roads to the Lura Lakes are not easily accessible between May and November and are in quite a bad state generally, a third of the route being

Peshkopi's main street with its brightly coloured buildings

unasphalted and requiring 4WD cars. The only recommended access route is via Rreshen, Kurbnesh and Krej Lura to Fushë Lura. Public transport is only sporadically available to villages near the park.

There's one simple but good hotel near the lakes, with a second one under construction at the time of writing. Both can be booked via the Hotel Turismi travel agency (*see pp148–9*), who can also arrange transport and guided trips.

Peshkopi

Cut off from its economic hinterland by the borders that were drawn following the disintegration of the Ottoman Empire, the town of Peshkopi in the east of Albania suffered deep isolation until the reopening of the borders in 1991. A charming place with a lively pedestrianised main street, a small Ottoman-era district, a bustling bazaar area and smiles all around, Peshkopi offers the full Albanian experience with not a tourist in sight. A beautiful but gruelling six-hour, 190km (118-mile) drive from Tirana, the town is set between lovely rolling hills with Mali Korabit (Mount Korabi), Albania's highest, towering in the background. At 650m (2,100ft) above sea level, temperatures in Peshkopi are moderate in summer and quite cold in winter.

You'll enter town near the bazaar, where you'll find the mosque and some old houses. Down the steps from the main street are countless stalls and workshops, and just down the road by the river is the fruit, vegetable and animal market. In scenes recalling the Wild West, people in traditional dress ride in on horseback from nearby villages, using woven baskets to transport all manner of goods to and from the market. Axes are ground, wood is sawed, tailors stitch clothes, lambs are tied up by their feet and slung bleating over bicycle handlebars, and sheep are slaughtered in the on-site abattoir. Beyond the old town area, the pleasant 1960s new town has a wide pedestrianised boulevard that is filled with people socialising. Just to the east of town, the *llixhat* (thermal baths) offer the opportunity to soak a while in water that reeks of sulphur.

Valbona

A rugged alpine valley with a river so beautiful that Albanian girls are named after it. Located 25km (15 miles) north of Bajram Curri in the isolated northeast of the country, Valbona offers beautiful mountain vistas. The wide expanse of the village centre is somewhat disfigured by an impressively ruined state hotel, though slightly lower down there's a lovely pocket of farmhouses and fields straight from a postcard.

It's possible to hire a guide to hike across the pass to Thethi, but you can also do day trips within the valley. It's an easy two-hour walk up the road to Rragam, the last village in the valley. A relatively easy five-hour hike leads to Mala e Rosit (Rose Mountain) with excellent views over to Montenegro, while a more demanding six-hour hike goes to the lakes below the peak of Mali i Jezercës (Mount Jezerca). Guides are necessary for these hikes.

The best time to visit Valbona is from June to mid-November, as snow levels can be high in winter, and half the local families move down to Bajram Curri during this period. The village is reached by daily *furgon* minibus from Bajram Curri, which connects to the early morning *furgon* buses coming from Tirana and takes just over an hour. Roads are good until just past Bajram Curri, after which normal cars can drive on to Valbona only at a very slow pace. Accommodation is available at a guesthouse in the quaint part of Valbona village.

Village houses in the Valbona Valley

When to go

Depending on what you want to do, Albania can be a year-round destination. You can bake on a beach in high summer, wander through the forests' golden foliage in autumn, join a guided snow-shoe trek through dazzling alpine landscapes in winter, or frolic around in fields full of wild flowers in spring. The good news: it's nearly always low season in Albania, and you'll often be the only foreigner for miles.

Climate

Coastal Albania has a typical Mediterranean climate, with stiflingly hot summers and cool winters. Average summer temperatures along the seaside vary from 18°C (64°F) at night to 30°C (86°F) during the day, though in July and August highs closer to 40°C (104°F) are possible. It seldom dips below freezing in winter, with averages of 14°C (57°F) in the afternoon. Rainy days are scarce in summer.

Venture away from the sea, and things change dramatically. Tirana and many other inland destinations are located well above sea level and between mountain ranges, with a continental climate characterised by slightly hotter summers and colder, wetter winters. Count on summer temperatures fluctuating between 17°C (63°F) at night and 31°C (88°F) by day – with extremes up to 38°C (100°F) – and winters between 2°C (36°F) at night and 13°C (55°F) by day. Deeper into Albania's mountainous interior, temperatures can be quite low even in high summer.

In summer, you'll only need to bring a light sweater or jacket for the cooler evenings and the occasional rainy day. If you plan to head to the mountain villages, bring an all-weather coat and

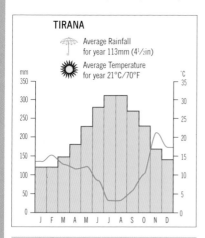

TIRANA

Average Rainfall
for year 113mm (4½in)

Average Temperature
for year 21°C/70°F

WEATHER CONVERSION CHART

25.4mm = 1 inch
°F = 1.8 × °C + 32

good shoes, and be prepared for cold nights and cool days. Winters are wet and foul, so winter coats and thick shoes are necessary, or full alpine gear if you're planning outdoor trips high in the mountains.

Tourist seasons

There are still so few foreign tourists in Albania that you could say it has a year-round low season, the only notable exception being the main beaches that get busy in June and are absolutely packed in July and August.

Without doubt, the best seasons to travel in Albania are spring and autumn. Temperatures in May and June are good for the beach (though the sea is still chilly) and perfect for hiking. The hillsides will be a riot of wild flowers and scents, and Spring is also the best season for food, as fresh produce returns to the local markets and restaurants after the sober winter months. The autumn months from September to early November are similarly pleasant, with empty beaches, warm seawater and stunning forest colours.

You'll find that the summer months July and August are often too hot for comfort, towns and villages become dusty and deserted in the stifling afternoon hours, simply walking around sights can feel like a marathon, and the frequent power cuts may mean that the hotel air conditioning doesn't work. Traffic along the coast is hectic in high summer with the influx of

Spring is a good time to visit Mount Dajti

thousands of emigrant Albanians and Kosovars. The hot weather is also bad for the quality of the seawater near the cities and for the general hygiene in restaurant kitchens. In the wet, cold winters there's mud in the city streets, and insufficient heating and insulation can make restaurants and hotels draughty and cold.

Getting around

Although Albania's transport sector is complete chaos in the eyes of most foreign visitors, it's actually quite easy and cheap to get around the country – though seldom comfortable – as long as you know the basic facts. The cheapest and often fastest way to get around the country is by bus and furgon, *the most popular modes of transport with locals. Although a second airport is planned at Kukës, Albania has no domestic flights as yet.*

Buses and *furgons*

Bus travel does come with a manual, as Albania still has no proper bus stations, scheduled departure times or advance ticket sales and the last bus often departs in the early afternoon. The main problem is finding out about departure locations and times, as these change all the time. You just have to ask around to find out the latest information. The good news is that the bus services are rapidly developing and improving, they're cheap, and they have friendly drivers and passengers who are always happy to help foreigners get to their final destination.

The most common type of bus is the *furgon* ('van'), a privately owned minibus seating 8 to 15 people and shuttling between two destinations a few times per day. *Furgons* can be stopped anywhere and often only depart when the driver feels he has enough passengers. *Furgon* travel can feel quite adventurous, with chickens, goats and pigs sometimes on board for rural rides, though drivers use Albanian driving techniques to negotiate the roads, which may make first-time visitors uneasy. Some busy routes, like Tirana to Durrës, have *furgons* departing several times per hour while other destinations have just one or two connections per day. Large buses are increasingly common on main routes in the coastal areas and on long-distance routes to the main cities. They're better at sticking to traffic rules than the *furgons* and are a bit slower as a result. As a rule you pay 150–200 lekë per hour of travel, so Tirana to Shkodra costs 300 lekë, and Tirana to Saranda (a six-hour trip) 1,200 lekë.

Trains

Albania's weary rail network is the only one in Europe that's not connected to other countries. Getting around by train is a very slow process, and the imported second-hand carriages used by Hekurudha Shqiptarë, the Albanian national railways, can be quite grotty.

A *furgon* minibus drives through the mountains

Nevertheless, if you're up for it, taking a train can be a cheap and revealing adventure. The most useful line is that between Tirana and Durrës, with four trains per day (five in summer) making the 45-minute trip. On all other routes, buses are much faster. The line between Elbasan and Pogradec, however, is worth mentioning for the magnificent mountain and lake views along the way, and for the high bridges the train crosses. Train tickets are sold just before departure, there's only one class and it's incredibly cheap.

Taxis

All cities have taxis that can be hailed on the street. Taxi meters are rare, so you'll have to agree a price in advance. A short ride in Tirana will set you back around 200–300 lekë, to the suburbs 400–500 lekë. Prices in other cities are slightly lower. Taxis are also useful for day trips to isolated sights and for getting to or across the border. It's a good idea to shop around to compare offers.

Bicycles

Albania is a great country for adventurous cycle trips, though there's no bike rental available anywhere yet so you'll need to bring your own or buy one locally. Cycling in the cities can be hazardous with the bad roads and haphazard driving. The flat city of Shkodra is the main exception: many people use bikes to get around and the municipality even recently built dedicated bike paths. Once you're away from the cities and main roads it's a pleasure to cycle around, though you'll always need to be vigilant for potholes and speeding drivers. Always lock your bike and remove all baggage and loose parts when parking it, and take it inside your hotel after dark. The best place to buy a bicycle in Albania is on Rruga Qemal Stafa near Tirana's central market, where there are a dozen small bike shops. Regular mountain-biking trips are organised by the Outdoor Albania travel agency (*see p145*).

Cars

Driving in Albania is the rally-enthusiast's dream and a prudent driver's nightmare. In 1991 there were only a few hundred cars in the whole country. Since then, everyone and his dog has imported a second-hand Mercedes and has seemingly learned to drive by trial and error. The traffic accident statistics are quite bad, with 25 deaths every month resulting from a combination of bad driving, bad roads and the peculiar mix of road users, which varies from livestock and drunken men on bikes to speeding Ferraris. That said, driving is the best way to make the most of a trip to Albania. The best advice is to keep your eyes peeled, keep your distance from other cars, and don't count on doing more than 50km/h (30mph). The main roads in Albania are all of good quality or undergoing major upgrading works. Secondary roads are often asphalted but can be very bumpy. Minor roads are often unsurfaced. A 4WD car is not necessary for

trips along the main roads but is recommended for visiting off-the-beaten-track destinations. Speed limits are 40km/h (25mph) in villages and urban areas, and 90km/h (56mph) on other roads, unless indicated otherwise. Police often use radar to check speeds.

Tirana has several international and local car rental agencies with city-centre offices and desks at the airport, often only open if they're expecting clients. They offer various types of cars, and pick-ups and drop-offs at borders or other towns are possible at a surcharge. Rental prices are aimed towards business travellers and are considerably higher than in Greece or Montenegro, so if you can take a rental car from abroad you may save money. Do check carefully if the agency allows this first. Petrol stations can be found in every town, with prices below Western European levels.

Ferries

The only major ferry connection in Albania, apart from the international ferries connecting Durrës and Vlora to Italy, is the car and passenger ferries crossing the spectacular Lake Koman, between Koman and Fierza (*see pp64–5*). The battered boat doesn't look very solid and is usually overloaded, but it's a fantastic trip and the alternative is a six-hour drive across atrocious mountain roads. It's a good idea to arrive early to be sure of a place on the ferry.

The view from the ferry on Lake Koman

Accommodation

With new hotels opening every month, Albania's hotel scene is rapidly improving. And with the exception of a few top-class hotels in Tirana, accommodation options in Albania remain, for at least the foreseeable future, ludicrously cheap, making choosing the right place to stay slightly more complicated than usual due to the fact that just about everything is affordable. Hotels and guesthouses range in quality from 5-star palaces complete with wireless Internet to spartan rooms with shared facilities.

Other options include some limited camping facilities in rural areas, some back-to-nature-style cabins plus a few youth hostels. Outside the capital, a single room in a clean and comfortable hotel complete with en-suite facilities will seldom set you back more than 2,500 lekë a night. Hotels often quote their prices in euros, but you're expected to pay in lek.

Where Albania continues to let the side down is in the quality of service and amenities on offer. These are somewhat comparable to the standards as they were shortly after independence in now much more advanced countries such as Poland and Slovenia. Just because every room comes with a Jacuzzi® doesn't necessarily mean there'll be hot water to put in it, for example. Neither should you imagine that the Internet connection in your room is going to work, that there'll be curtains in an east-facing room, nor for that matter that anyone will remember to do your laundry.

Arrive at a seaside resort hotel on a hot day in June, and you may find that they have not bothered to clean or even fill the swimming pool yet. On the plus side, Albanian hospitality is second to none, making all those little quirks much more palatable. Some flexibility and patience on your part will go a long way to helping you enjoy your trip. That said, asking for a partial refund is perfectly warranted in such situations.

During the high summer season, rooms on the Albanian Riviera fill up fast, but elsewhere room capacity is still larger than demand and you won't have to worry about finding a place to stay on arrival. If you want to stay at a specific hotel, however, it's worth calling in advance. The lack of reliable Internet connections and the Albanian propensity to underestimate the importance of marketing makes booking accommodation in advance harder than in any other country in Europe. Independent publications are also thin on the ground, and it's been left to guidebooks such as this one and the excellent and growing *In Your Pocket* city guides to Albanian destinations (*www.inyourpocket.com*) to fill the gap. The website *www.albania-hotel.com*, run by a local travel agent, has a good overview of bookable options throughout the country too. More and more travel companies are offering organised trips to Albania, and

their services should be pre-booked before departure by those who need their basic needs catered to. Even if you have booked a room before you arrive, remember that finding a hotel can be tricky as street names are rare and many hotels simply don't list an address (*see p28*). Hotels are often used as points of reference by the locals, so asking around when you're in town usually guarantees success.

The Livia Hotel in Butrint, adjacent to the archaeological site

Food and drink

Mediterranean, fresh, simple and healthy – Albanian food is surprisingly good and varied, and like many aspects of this country it's heavily influenced by its Balkan neighbours, notably Greece and Turkey. Unlike in many Western countries, food is still quite seasonal here and travelling in spring when the first good fruit and vegetables reappear on menus is a delight. Albania's poor agricultural sector has little money for pesticides so most food here is organic and free of chemicals.

Breakfast in hotels is a simple affair, usually with bread or toast, an omelette, cheese and cold meats with tea, coffee or juice. Even mid-range hotels often have quite disappointing breakfasts, so don't raise your hopes. Lunch and dinner are a different matter, and Albanians take their time for a good meal. The good news is that meals in Albania are still very cheap by Western standards. Imported cuisine and special fresh fish are the exception.

Albanian meals are centred around meat dishes, supplemented by salads, beans, bread, potatoes, french fries or rice. *Qofta*, a small grilled meat patty that is sometimes flavoured with mint, is eaten as a snack with bread and fresh chopped onion and washed down with *kos*, a yoghurt drink, or *salce kosi*, a yoghurt dish similar to *tzatziki*. Korça has its own variety of *qofta*, logically called *qofta Korça*, which consists of meatballs in a tasty tomato sauce. *Shish qebab* skewers and *sufflaqa* or *pita* (döner kebab) are another main staple.

Oven dishes include *tave*, a small earthenware pot with a mix of meat, feta cheese and yoghurt, and peppers, aubergines and other vegetables stuffed with ground meat and rice. This country of mountains and shepherds has excellent lamb – look for *paidhaqe*, grilled lamb ribs. *Byrek*, a triangular flaky pastry filled with cheese, spinach or meat, is a typical Balkan dish that can be found sold in special shops (*byrektore*) across the country. *Bakllava*, a filling, sticky pastry with sugary water and nuts, is available as dessert but is more often eaten as a snack.

Affordable fish restaurants abound near the coast and lakes, serving *kocë* (sea bream), *levrek* (sea bass) and specialities like *koran* trout around Lake Ohrid and delicious *ngjalë* (eels) near the lagoons and rivers. The best fish restaurants are usually found right beside the sea, lake or river where the fish are caught, though Tirana also has a selection of seafood places. Salads in Albania are fresh and delicious and you can't go wrong with a *sallat grek* consisting of tomatoes, cucumber, onions, feta cheese, olives and olive oil.

Variety in restaurants is still rather small, with the majority serving Albanian food together with Italian dishes like pasta and pizza. It's only in Tirana that there's a real choice, with reasonable authentic Chinese, French, Mexican, Indian, Turkish and Japanese cuisine all represented now. If you're on a long trip, it's a good idea to splash out on exotic food in Tirana while you have the chance.

All is not lost for vegetarians, as there are several Albanian dishes without meat that you can order, as well as the salads of course, though it may become tedious after a week or two. Many restaurants have vegetarian pizza on the menu, or can leave out the meat on request. Self-catering vegetarians can find everything they need at the daily food markets or street stalls available in all towns, which have fresh fruit, vegetables, cheese and other items. It's easy to shop for a picnic or to fill your hotel fridge with healthy snacks.

Beer, *raki* and coffee are the most popular drinks in Albania. Well-known local beer brands are Birra Tirana and

A *byrek* seller in Vlora

Lunchtime salad and bread at a mountain guesthouse

Locally bottled mineral water is cheap and widely available, and this country of mountains and springs has plenty of variety, the biggest brands being Glina and Tepelena (with its memorable warped English slogan on the label: 'Suffled how it gush from the source of the woods of Tepelena'). Increasingly, restaurants will import bottled water from Italy or France and you'll pay through the nose for it.

Good restaurants can be found in towns as well as along main roads and in popular tourist destinations, and it's quite possible that your most memorable meal will be in some scruffy nameless tavern out in the sticks rather than in a swanky Tirana eatery. Eating out in restaurants is no different from elsewhere, though there are some quirks to contend with. Restaurant staff usually intend well but often come across as over-zealous or completely incompetent, and you'll probably repeatedly have to remind waiters to bring you cutlery, salt, serviettes and sometimes also the food you ordered. Some waiters also have a habit of disappearing for long periods of time. This is easily solved if you wander into the kitchen to remind him of the work at hand. Restaurant menus in the cities are often available in English, though elsewhere you may have to ask for a translation or gamble. Small-town restaurants often have very limited choice and it's best to ask what the waiter recommends. Many restaurants are family-run, and especially away

Birra Korça, though imported beer is widely available. *Raki*, the surprisingly strong local firewater, is distilled from grapes, plums or other fruit such as mulberries, and is often taken as an appetiser. Albanian wine is good but often hard to find in restaurants, though increased production and marketing should soon mean there's more choice. In Tirana there are several wine bars that have a wide variety of local and foreign wines. Coffee is the fuel that Albania really runs on, and you'll see people drinking it at all times of day. The Italian varieties are widely available, though it's fun to try the traditional *kafee turke* once; it's made by pouring hot water directly onto ground coffee. It's a good idea to wait a while between stirring and drinking this.

from the main cities they'll be delighted to see foreigners and will do their best to make you comfortable. Instead of saying that something is out of stock, you'll often see an uneasy-looking waiter sent scurrying to the nearest shop or supermarket to fetch some missing ingredients or the can of cola that you ordered. If you're in a hurry, it's best to head for a pizzeria or a place selling snacks rather than counting on a restaurant to feed you quickly.

Many restaurants operate all day without official opening hours, starting early in the morning between 6am and 9am to serve coffee to people on their way to work, and closing around 10pm or 11pm after the last customers leave.

Olives for sale at the central market in Tirana

123

Food and drink

Entertainment

You would think that Albania's tough history and deep poverty would affect the capability of people to have fun, but you'll be amazed that even without all the hi-tech entertainment options available to us in the West, Albanians manage to seem all the more happy to simply use the streets to mingle, chat and drink coffee with friends. That said, with the economic boom, modern entertainment options have recently appeared.

Cafés and restaurants

The best entertainment available in Albania, to locals and foreigners alike, is offered for free on the streets. The evening *xhiro*, when everyone comes out to chat, offers great people-watching and socialising opportunities at any of the many roadside cafés.

Mall cinema in Tirana

In summer, when the emigrants come home for a month, it's easy to pick up conversation here, and the best news is that Albanians make good and cheap coffee. Going to a restaurant is still somewhat of a luxury for most people, and in some towns the choice in food is rather limited, though with the economic advances, an increasing number of locals can afford to eat out. Often, the best traditional Albanian restaurant in town will have live music on weekend evenings. Saturday is wedding day and you'll find many restaurants crammed full with eating and dancing people – and you may just get invited in to join the fun.

Cinema and stage performances

Decent cinemas showing Hollywood productions can be found in most cities, with Albania's first multiplex under construction at the time of writing. For art-house films your only hope is the Akademia e Filmit & Multimedias Marubi (Academy of

Shkodra's Migjeni Theatre

Film and Multimedia Marubi, *see p144*), which has free weekly screenings of foreign films. Films are subtitled and not dubbed in Albania. Theatre performances are held in most cities but are almost exclusively in Albanian. If there's a foreign group visiting, there will be posters announcing the event. Catching an opera or ballet show is usually only possible in Tirana, where your hotel should be able to find out what's on.

Cultural events

Albania has plenty of folk festivals and outdoor concerts in the warmer months, and foreigners are welcome to join in the festivities if they happen to chance upon a party. Small festivals, handicrafts fairs and concerts are held throughout the country, and asking around is still the best way to get to know about such events. The annual **Mjaft Fest** (*www.mjaftfest.com*) music

festival is aimed at young people from across Europe and attracts bands from the Balkans and beyond.

Nightlife

Western-style bars are relatively new to Albania, as cafés did a good job of serving alcoholic drinks until now. Now that young people have a little money in their pockets, modern bars serving everything from beer and *raki* to cocktails are starting to appear, some of the nicer ones run by Albanians who learned the trade in London or New York. Some bars will put on live music, though there's no good way to find out about these events except by looking for posters or asking around. Tirana has a modest club scene, though in summer many clubs close shop, some of them moving their parties to the beach at Durrës. Dress up if you plan to go out: Albanians look their best when they go to bars and clubs.

Shopping

A veritable retail boom has hit Albania in recent years. The country that once had only dour state-owned shops with empty shelves and endless queues for the most basic items like sugar, milk and bread now has lively shopping streets with small boutiques and an increasing number of modern shopping malls. Tourists looking for souvenirs have a limited but good selection of handicrafts to choose from.

Popular Albanian souvenirs include traditional folk dress and woven items, carved wooden plates and statues of the national hero Skanderbeg. The Albanian flag with its characteristic black two-headed eagle on a red background is also available on T-shirts and other objects. The small marble

Handmade children's cots for sale in Shkodra

ashtrays shaped like bunkers make a very novel present. Most towns have one or two dedicated souvenir shops in the centre, though there are also stands on the streets, like in Berat's citadel area and at the southern end of Rruga Barrikadave in Tirana. The bazaar in Kruja may have the best selection in the country, also selling antiques and other old-looking items. The airport, too, has a good souvenir shop.

When it comes to shopping for clothes and shoes, you must realise that Albania has just recently acquired a middle class and consumerism has yet to reach Western levels. But now that the country has changed from an impoverished importer of cheap second-hand goods into an exporter of quality clothes and shoes, mainly to the Italian market, there are some bargains to be had. Predictably, Tirana has the best range of shops in the country, many of them in the city's Bllok area. There is a quite astonishing range of good-quality shoes available

The Galeria, a modern shopping mall in Tirana

in the dozens of footwear boutiques in Tirana's city centre, with prices much lower than in other Eastern European cities. Modern clothing boutiques also abound, though tall Western Europeans may find sizes tailored too much towards the somewhat shorter Albanians. Apart from the Bllok area, the best mix of shoe and fashion shops is found along Rruga Myslym Shyri, just to the west of Rinia Park.

English-language books are hard to come by, but Tirana's **Adrion Bookshop** (*Sheshi Skënderbej, inside the Pallatin e Kulturës (Palace of Culture) building*) has the country's best selection of Albania-related books. There's a good range of history books about Albania and the region, as well as beautifully published photo books such

as *Albania from the Air* by Alket Islami, which has fantastic low-altitude aerial photos taken from a motorised parasail.

Although the fresh produce is delicious in Albania, it's difficult to take home without squashing, and it may be illegal to import elsewhere anyway. Honey and home made jams (including exotic tastes like figs) and dried fruits are all sold at local markets and make great presents. Alcohol-lovers might like to take home a liquid souvenir, and there's no better way to remember all those blurry evenings than by fondly opening a bottle of Albania's local poison, *raki*. A bottle won't cost much at all, and a range of brands can be found at any good supermarket. Alternatively, try the unlabelled home-distilled varieties available at markets.

Sport and leisure

Albania may be rich in natural beauty with its mountains, plains and stunning coastline, but the development of sports and leisure activities has only just begun. Travellers interested in outdoor activities have little choice, with only one good outdoor sports specialist in the country and few other initiatives. Spectator sports are easier to find, with football the most popular activity.

Beach sports and activities

Many of the more popular beaches offer waterskiing, jetskiing and boat rental, but these are often haphazard operations with little attention to safety. Scuba diving is good in the south of the country, especially around Vlora's bay where there are some good wrecks, but as there's no dive centre in Albania yet you'll have to bring your own gear from abroad. If you do plan to dive, be aware of military areas where you may need permits first. Snorkelling around the rocky headlands of the Albanian Riviera is good, with clear waters and plenty of fish and other aquatic life. Good snorkelling gear is scarce in Albania so, again, you'll need to bring your own.

Outdoor activities

Albania really shines as an outdoor sports destination. The rugged roads and paths of the mountainous interior are perfect for hiking, mountain biking and 4WD tours. In spring the mountain streams turn into raging rivers that are great for wild-water rafting. In winter the high ranges offer pristine ski touring and snow-shoe trekking, though there are no facilities anywhere for downhill skiing. Some persistent ski fanatics trudge up the slopes at Voskopoja and other mountain areas to zip down again, but the nearest proper skiing is to be found in neighbouring Kosovo, Montenegro and Greece. The rocky coastline of the south is perfect for sea kayaking. At the moment, the problem is that the tourism infrastructure is still largely absent, with few operators offering services. For an active holiday in Albania, contact Tirana-based Outdoor Albania (*see p145*), which can arrange short and long trips involving any of the above sports. Hiking can be done without the help of a local operator, though the absence of good maps and route markings makes this inadvisable for absolute beginners. The area around Thethi is wonderful for hiking, and you can leave the area by hiking across a

Visiting in winter gives you the opportunity to try snow-shoe trekking in the Albanian Alps

pass to Valbona. Local guides can be hired in Thethi and Valbona for about 1,900–3,100 lekë per day, depending on distance and difficulty.

Spectator sports

Apart from during the summer season when all team sports are on hold, there are plenty of sports events you can attend. Football is Albania's most popular sport. The Albanian national football team is reasonably successful and plays home matches in Tirana's Qemal Stafa stadium on Sheshi Italia. Tirana has two teams, Dinamo and KF Tirana, the latter of which plays at Tirana's other stadium, Selman

Stërmasi on Rruga Sulejman Delvina. Football match tickets can be purchased at the stadium ticket offices in the days before the match. Handball, volleyball and other indoor sports competitions are also popular, and most towns will have noticeboards near the town hall or on the main street that announce matches.

Swimming

The only good public swimming pool is the Aquadrom complex (*see p130*) near the Grand Park in Tirana. Many of the new hotels and some restaurants along the coast or near cities have pools that guests can use.

Children

Foreign visitors to Albania can generally expect a warm welcome, and as children are universally adored, they'll be patted and smiled at continuously. Although Albania lacks the large-scale commercial initiatives apparently needed to keep them happy back home, there are plenty of things that will have your little ones fascinated. Some city hotels now have family rooms and suites, and children are welcome in most restaurants. And car rental agencies offer chauffeured minibuses that are ideal for larger families.

Most types of nappies and baby food are now available at Albania's better supermarkets, though you're best to bring a supply of your own if you want a specific type. Be aware that pavements can be bumpy and kerbs high, so consider taking a sturdy pushchair with big wheels. The summer sun and heat can be very strong, so bring along the appropriate sunblocks and consider noontime siestas.

Aquadrom

Escape Tirana's summer heat in the city's water-sports complex, with four pools, plenty of slides, a café and generally good facilities.
Near the Grand Park. Tel: (04) 225 6257. Open: May–Oct 9am–7pm.

Beaches

If your children prefer to muck around with sand rather than pebbles, stick to the beaches north of Vlora, or head to Ksamil in the south. Older children may enjoy snorkelling and poking around rocks, and for them the Riviera beaches will be perfect.

Castles

Nothing fascinates young children more than dramatically situated castles, and Albania has several. Near to Tirana, it's easy to visit Petrela Castle (*see p30*), a picture-perfect semi-ruin perched on a high rock with a good restaurant. The citadel at Kruja (*see p37*) is also close by and offers the added benefit of containing the interesting Ethnographic Museum. Finally, the large castles in Shkodra (*see pp60–61*) and Berat (*see pp48–50*) are great for romping around with the kids. At all castles, watch out for unmarked steep drops.

Fairground rides

Every city in Albania will have a few fairground rides along the local *xhiro* route in the evenings when whole families come out to chat and relax. In front of Tirana's National History

Splashing around at Lake Ohrid

Museum, the place where Enver Hoxha's statue used to stand is now a small racetrack for children's electric cars. The sea-front promenades in Vlora and Durrës sometimes have quite impressive rides for adults, too. In Tirana, there's a modest but fun permanent fairgound with bumper cars, trampolines, a rollercoaster and various other attractions, costing very little per ride (*Corner of Blvd Bajram Curri & Rruga Elbasanit; open: 4–10pm*).

Teatri i Kukullave (Puppet Theatre)

Tirana's puppet theatre has weekly productions aimed at young children. Although they're sometimes performed with spoken Albanian text, foreign children will probably be delighted with the show anyway.

Sheshi Austria, off Sheshi Skënderbej, Tirana. Tel: (04) 222 2446. Admission charge.

Village stays

Nothing beats a stay on a real farm, with pigs, chickens, ducks and geese running free. Treat the children to an educational stay at a family guesthouse in Albania's northern mountains, for instance in Thethi or Vermoshi. The host family will be happy to let children help a bit with farm work by feeding the animals, sowing and ploughing with the horse. For information on guesthouses in northern Albania, contact GTZ in Shkodra (*see pp58–9*).

Essentials

Arriving

By air

Tirana International Airport (TIA), officially Nënë Tereza (Mother Teresa) airport, is the country's only international airport, some 17km (10½ miles) northwest of the capital. In 2007 a much-needed new terminal was opened. The airport serves around 33 destinations in Europe. British Airways (*www.britishairways.com*) flies to Tirana from London Gatwick, and Albanian Airlines (*www.albanianairlines.com.al*) operates a flight from London Stansted. Budget airlines are currently limited to flights to Italy and Germany (see *www.whichbudget.com* for the latest information). The cheapest way to get to the city centre is in the Rinas Express bus, which leaves hourly between 8am and 7pm, arriving beside the National Museum. A one-way ticket costs 250 lekë. Avoid illegal taxis by using the yellow Airport Express taxis (*tel: (04) 223 3419*), which charge a reasonable 2,100–2,500 lekë for the 30–45-minute drive.
Tirana International Airport.
Tel: (04) 37 9063. www.tirana-airport.com

By sea

Albania has car ferry links with Italy, which are particularly busy in summer when thousands of emigrant Albanians return home (*www.cemar.it*). Ferries arrive at Durrës and Vlora. Corfu in Greece has a daily passenger ferry to Saranda, with additional hydrofoil services to Saranda and Himara in summer (*www.ionian-cruises.com*).

By land

Albania's land border crossings have been dramatically improved and expanded in the past decade, and it's now possible to enter Albania at dozens of points. The main border crossings are at Hani i Hotit, between Shkodra and Podgorica in Montenegro, at Qafe e Thanës between Elbasan and Ohrid in Macedonia and at Kakavija between Gjirokastra and Ioannina in Greece. Border formalities are usually dealt with efficiently, and outside the busy summer period you should be able to cross over in 15–30 minutes. Note that the Albanian railway network is not connected to other countries, so public cross-border transport is limited to buses.

Customs

You can bring 200 cigarettes, 1 litre of spirits and 2 litres of wine into Albania, but you would be mad to do so as these items are all very cheap locally. Exporting antiques and precious metals requires export permits that can be obtained from the licensed sellers.

Electricity

Electricity in Albania is 240V AC. Sockets are standard European two-pin.

Bring an adaptor with you as they're almost impossible to find anywhere in the country. Occasional power cuts occur, so carrying a small torch or lighter is a wise precaution. Bring a candle or two if you're staying in the countryside.

Internet

Most towns have at least one Internet café, charging a small amount per hour, while in Tirana many cafés and restaurants have Wi-Fi, though the quality of the connection is often bad. Outside of Tirana, most accommodation doesn't come with Internet. Dodgy connections and power cuts also mean that just because a place does have Internet access there's no guarantee it's going to work.
Vodafone Albania (*www.vodafone.al*)

also provides a mobile Internet service.

Money

The Albanian currency is the lek (plural lekë) and is divided into 100, as good as obsolete, *qindarka*. Notes come in denominations of 5,000, 1,000, 500, 200 and 100 lekë, and coins in denominations of 50, 20, 10, 5, 2 and 1 lekë. To curb inflation, a zero was knocked off the lek a few years back, and many people continue to refer to money as if the zero were still there. Before you express outrage at the price of a bar of chocolate, make sure you've been quoted the price using the new currency. Lekë can't be exchanged outside of Albania, so spend them all before leaving. The best way to get lekë is by using ATMs, which are fairly

Tirana's yellow taxis are found at stands or can be hailed on the street

A colourful government building in Tirana

around 10pm. City-centre restaurants may stay open longer than that. Banking hours are from 8am or 9am to 3pm Monday to Friday.

Passports, visas and entry fees

Visas are not required for citizens of the UK, USA, Canada, Australia, New Zealand and most other Western countries. South Africans and all others need to apply for a visa in advance from an Albanian embassy, a list of which can be found at *www.mfa.gov.al*. Most foreigners need to pay an entry tax on arrival, which is €10 at the airport or €1 at land or sea borders. Payment in other major currencies is possible. There is no departure tax. Passports need to be valid for six months from the date of entry.

Pharmacies

You'll find a *barnatore* or *farmaci* (pharmacy) in all towns, most of them modern and well equipped and with generous opening hours. Staff are knowledgeable but English may not be spoken so bring an Albanian speaker along if you require special medicines. It's best to bring anything you may need from abroad with you. The **Farmaci Regi dhe Bime Mjeksore** (*Rruga Dëshmorët e 4 Shkurtit; tel: (04) 222 6759*) in Tirana's Bllok area is on duty round the clock.

Post

All towns have post offices run by **Posta Shqiptare** (*www.postashqiptare.al*).

widespread now, some offering a choice of lekë and euros. If you need to change money, your best option is to use a bank or an official exchange office. Credit cards are increasingly accepted in up-market hotels and shops in the main cities, but it's still wise to carry cash at all times, as most places in Albania are strictly cash-only. Haggling is quite acceptable in many places.

Opening hours

Shops are usually open Monday to Saturday between 8am and 7pm and, unlike in other Mediterranean countries, do not close for lunch. Restaurants often double as cafés and open very early, between 6am and 8am, closing late at night after the last customers leave, which is usually

Mailing a postcard or letter within Europe costs 60 lekë, outside Europe 80 lekë. The mail service is generally dependable, but it may take a week or two for mail to arrive. For important and valuable mailings, it's best to use an express mail company.

Public holidays

Apart from the general public holidays, Albania celebrates the holidays of all three religions, including *Big Bajram*, celebrated a day after the end of Ramadan, and the sacrifice feast *Kurban Bajram* 69 days later.

1 January New Year's Day
14 March Summer Day
22 March Islamic New Year (Nevrus Day)
March/April Catholic and Orthodox Easter (on different days in spring)
1 May May Day
19 October Mother Teresa Day (celebrating her beatification)
28–9 November Independence Day and Liberation Day
25 December Christmas Day

Smoking

The Albanians are some of the heaviest smokers in Europe. In 2007 the Albanian government banned smoking in all public buildings including bars and restaurants, a law that seems impossible to enforce. Most popular brands of cigarettes are available and extremely cheap to buy.

Suggested reading and media
Books
Broken April by Ismail Kadare.
A chilling story of blood revenge in the northern mountains.
High Albania by Edith Durham.
A classic account of Albania in the throes of uprising against the Ottomans. Highly recommended.
Rumpalla by Peter Lucas.
Albania seen through the eyes of an American journalist who visited several times in the 1980s.
The Albanians: A Modern History by Miranda Vickers.
An excellent book about the country's recent history.

Newspapers
Albanian Daily News.
www.albaniannews.com
The Tirana Times.
www.tiranatimes.com

Websites
www.albaniantourism.com
the official tourism website
www.albania-hotel.com
the only local hotel booking website
www.argjiro.net/fjalor
an online Albanian–English dictionary
www.elsie.de
translated Albanian literature, poetry and early photography
www.enverhoxha.info/frame.htm
a curious pro-Hoxha website
www.inyourpocket.com
free online and downloadable city guides to various destinations

www.poehali.org/en
detailed, downloadable Soviet-era military maps of Albania, useful for hiking
www.setimes.com
news from Albania and the region

Tax

VAT is included in all prices in shops, hotels and restaurants. The nasty habit of adding a certain percentage for service has not yet arrived in Albania, and customers are completely free to decide if they want to reward the waiter with any financial incentive.

Telephones

Public telephones are found in all towns and cities and accept cards that can be purchased at kiosks and post offices. Old men standing by the phones offer the use of their phone cards in exchange for a slightly inflated price, but it's easier than buying your own card first. Using your mobile phone in Albania is possible, though check with your provider to be sure yours will work. Business travellers who want to stay in touch via the Internet should bring a GPRS-enabled mobile phone or smart phone and call the local service provider for connection instructions. To save on the considerable costs of roaming, it's easy to buy a local AMC or Vodafone SIM card for using in your mobile phone. You'll need ID and a local address (a hotel suffices) to register your card.

International country codes: Australia *61*, Canada *1*, Ireland *353*, New Zealand *64*, South Africa *27*, UK *44*, US *1*.

To phone Albania, dial the international access code (usually *00*) + country code (*355*) + area code or mobile number (minus the initial zero)

The Ottoman bridge at Mesi, near Shkodra

Essentials

+ local number. Main Albania city area codes: Durrës *52*, Elbasan *545*, Korça *824*, Tirana *42*. Mobile numbers in Albania begin with *068* or *069*.

Time

Local time is GMT + one hour. The UK and Republic of Ireland are one hour behind, the Americas are six to nine hours behind and Australasia is about nine hours ahead. Clocks go forward an hour on the last Sunday of March and back again on the last Sunday of October.

Toilets

Public toilets don't exist in Albania. Nearly all restaurants and hotels have Western sit-down toilets now, and if you ask nicely you'll be allowed to use them. Not all of them have toilet paper, so it's a good idea to carry an emergency stash on you when you're on the road.

Travellers with disabilities

Some up-market hotels may have facilities for users of wheelchairs, but otherwise Albania presents a formidable steeplechase for the travellers with disabilities. The uneven pavements and absence of pedestrian street crossings don't make things easier. It is best to go with an organised group and to be clear about your needs when booking hotels and restaurants. For current information, contact RADAR, *12 City Forum, 250 City Rd, London EC1V 8AF. Tel: 020 7250 3222. www.radar.org.uk*

CONVERSION TABLE

FROM	TO	MULTIPLY BY
Inches	Centimetres	2.54
Feet	Metres	0.3048
Yards	Metres	0.9144
Miles	Kilometres	1.6090
Acres	Hectares	0.4047
Gallons	Litres	4.5460
Ounces	Grams	28.35
Pounds	Grams	453.6
Pounds	Kilograms	0.4536
Tons	Tonnes	1.0160

To convert back, for example from centimetres to inches, divide by the number in the third column.

MEN'S SUITS

UK	36	38	40	42	44	46	48
Rest of Europe	46	48	50	52	54	56	58
USA	36	38	40	42	44	46	48

DRESS SIZES

UK	8	10	12	14	16	18
France	36	38	40	42	44	46
Italy	38	40	42	44	46	48
Rest of Europe	34	36	38	40	42	44
USA	6	8	10	12	14	16

MEN'S SHIRTS

UK	14	14.5	15	15.5	16	16.5	17
Rest of Europe	36	37	38	39/40	41	42	43
USA	14	14.5	15	15.5	16	16.5	17

MEN'S SHOES

UK	7	7.5	8.5	9.5	10.5	11
Rest of Europe	41	42	43	44	45	46
USA	8	8.5	9.5	10.5	11.5	12

WOMEN'S SHOES

UK	4.5	5	5.5	6	6.5	7
Rest of Europe	38	38	39	39	40	41
USA	6	6.5	7	7.5	8	8.5

Language

Albanian is an ancient Indo-European language that's also spoken in Kosovo and parts of Macedonia and Montenegro and elsewhere. A curious language, Albanian has two dialects: Gheg, which is spoken in the north and in Kosovo and Macedonia, and Tosk, which is spoken in the south. Unlike in English, words in Albanian can be inflected depending upon gender and number, which explains the various spellings of city names you'll come across, and the definite article ('the') is stuck to the end of nouns. Over the ages, Albanian has also absorbed many words from other cultures, including Greek, Latin, Slavic and Turkish. English is widely spoken by the younger generation of Albanians, while knowledge of Greek and Italian is also generally good.

PRONUNCIATION

ç – as in 'check'
dh – as in 'the'
ë – as in 'fern'
g – as in 'get'
gj – as in 'cage'
j – as in 'yes'
nj – as in 'onion'
q – as 'check'
rr – as a trilled 'r'
x as in 'judge'
y as in 'muesli'

NUMBERS

0	zero
1	një
2	dy
3	tre
4	katër
5	pesë
6	gjashtë
7	shtatë
8	tetë
9	nëntë
10	dhjetë
100	njëqind
1,000	një mijë

BASIC WORDS AND PHRASES

Yes	Po
No	Jo
Please	Ju lutem
Thank you	Faleminderit
Excuse me	Më falni
Sorry	Më vjen keq
Hello	Tungjatjeta, tung
Good morning	Mirëmëngjes
Good day	Mirëdita
Good night	Natën e mirë
How are you?	Si jeni?
Cheers!	Gëzuar!
Today	Sot
Tomorrow	Nesër
Yesterday	Dje
Where?	Ku?
When?	Kur?
What?	Çfarë?
Why?	Pse?
Here	Këtu
Now	Tani
There	Atje
What's your name?	Si quheni?
My name is...	Unë quhem...
How much does this cost?	Sa kushton?

I don't speak Albanian	Nuk flas shqip
I don't understand	Nuk kuptoj
Open	Hapur
Closed	Mbyllur

IN THE RESTAURANT

Beef	Mish lope
Chicken	Zog pule
Lamb	Qengj
Pork	Mish derri
Sausage	Salam, suzhuk
Veal	Mish viçi
Schnitzel	Shnicel
Fish	Peshk
Prawns	Karkalec deti
Salmon	Salmon
Seafood	Fruta deti
Trout	Troftë
Apple	Mollë
Mushrooms	Kërpudhë
Orange	Portokalle
Peppers	Speca
Tomatoes	Domate
Beer	Birre
Juice	Leng
Wine	Verë
Water	Ujë
Waiter!	Kamarier!
A table for two	Një tavolin për dy
Non-smoking/ smoking	Ndalohet duhani/ Lejohet duhani
The menu, please	Menyn ju lutem
I'd like to order	Do doja ta bëja porosin
The bill, please	Faturën ju lutem
Where can I find a taxi?	Ku mund ta gjej një taksi?

DAYS AND MONTHS

Monday	E hëne
Tuesday	E marte
Wednesday	E mërkurë
Thursday	E enjte
Friday	E premte
Saturday	E shtunë
Sunday	E diel

January	Janar
February	Shkurt
March	Mars
April	Prill
May	Maj
June	Qershor
July	Korrik
August	Gusht
September	Shtator
October	Tetor
November	Nëntor
December	Dhjetor

Emergencies

Police	*42 19*
Ambulance	*42 17*
Fire	*42 18*

Embassies

Australia

The embassy in Athens provides consular assistance to Australian citizens. *Tel: + 30 21 087 040 00.* *www.greece.embassy.gov.au*

Canada

The embassy in Rome provides consular assistance to Canadian citizens. *Tel: + 39 06 854 442 911.* *www.dfait-maeci.gc.ca*

South Africa

The embassy in Rome provides consular assistance to South African citizens. *Tel: + 39 06 852 541. www.sudafrica.it*

UK

Rruga Skënderbej 12, Tirana. *Tel: (04) 223 4973. www.uk.al*

USA

Rruga Elbasanit 103, Tirana. *Tel: (04) 224 7285.* *http://tirana.usembassy.gov*

Health care

Western-quality health care is limited in Albania's underfunded health sector, though the doctors are well trained. A few good clinics equipped for emergencies and providing English-speaking staff can be found in Tirana, including the following:

ABC Clinic. *Rruga Qemal Stafa 260. Tel: (04) 223 4105.*
DSF Medical Centre. *Rruga Irfan Tomini 5. Tel: (04) 223 2799.*
Orthodox Clinic. *Rruga Dibres 159. Tel: (04) 236 0925.*

Health risks

No inoculations are required for Albania, though it's wise to get the standard ones (typhoid, Hepatitis A/B,

Make sure your travel insurance covers you if you want to try rafting

tuberculosis) up to date if you plan to visit isolated rural areas where hygiene may be a problem. Check the Albania recommendations at *www.mdtravelhealth.com* or ask your doctor for advice well before departure. In high summer, be careful to avoid sunburn and dehydration by using good sunscreen and protective clothing, and be sure to drink plenty of water. Tap water is usually fine to drink but doesn't taste great, so stick to mineral water, which is cheap and widely available. Stomach problems are the main worry for foreigners. You may need time to get used to the olive oil used in cooking, and in the hot summer, only order food that is freshly made. If you have stomach pain and diarrhoea, take rehydration salts and anti-diarrhoea medicine, but seek medical advice if it lasts more than a few days, becomes severe or is accompanied by fever.

Insurance

It's important to have travel and medical insurance before you go, as very serious accidents or illnesses will require evacuation. Check policies carefully for coverage of medical expenses, loss of baggage, repatriation, etc.

Police

Albania's yellow-vested police force can usually be found directing traffic away from the *xhiro* streets in the evenings, aiming radar devices at cars along the main roads, or sitting in cafés having a coffee. If you need to report a theft or other incident, it's best to take an Albanian speaker along.

Safety

Albania is perfectly safe to travel around now. The 1990s were a chaotic time in the country and travel warnings from that period can still be read occasionally, but are no longer relevant. Violent crimes against foreigners are very rare, as are muggings. Do watch out for pickpockets on beaches and when using public transport. Using a special hidden wallet or money belt for your passport and credit cards is a good idea in any unfamiliar country. In cities, keep expensive cameras and money hidden. The main worry should be the traffic in Albania, as accident statistics are very high. Avoid driving at night and always be aware of oncoming traffic driving in your lane, especially on bends.

Scams

Unlike many other European countries, scams aimed at tourists are scarce in Albania, mainly because of the absence of mass tourism from abroad. Drivers of *furgon* minibuses, shopkeepers and others are usually honest and will not try to rip off unsuspecting foreigners. By being careful when accepting help or drinks from strangers (though in Albania it's most likely to be honestly meant) and by changing money at banks rather than on the streets, you should stay clear of any scams.

Directory

Accommodation price guide

Prices are based on a standard double room per night, including breakfast.

★	under 5,000 lekë
★★	5,000–12,000 lekë
★★★	12,000–24,000 lekë
★★★★	over 24,000 lekë

Eating out price guide

The price ranges below indicate the price of a meal per person, without drinks.

★	under 500 lekë
★★	500–700 lekë
★★★	700–1,000 lekë
★★★★	over 1,000 lekë

TIRANA AND AROUND

Kruja

ACCOMMODATION

Panorama ★

A cheap and good place to spend the night if you don't want to make Kruja just a day trip. The Panorama is right beside the old bazaar and offers great views over the city. There's a good restaurant, too, if all you need is a meal.

Kruja bazaar.
Tel: (0511) 309 2. www. hotelpanorama-kruje.com

Tirana

ACCOMMODATION

Parlamenti ★

A cheap and cheerful family-run hotel along a small street just off Rruga Presidenti George W Bush, and indeed near the parliament building. It's central, clean and quiet and the top rooms have good views over an old part of town.

Rruga Jeronim de Rada 75.
Tel: (04) 226 5024.

Tirana Backpacker Hostel ★

The bunk beds in this charming yellow villa offer the cheapest sleep in town. There's a nice garden for relaxing and barbecuing, and the hostel staff is very friendly, regularly going clubbing with guests. The TBH also has an office of the Outdoor Albania adventure travel agency on site, and runs a summer hostel in Vuno, near Dhërmi on the Riviera coast.

Rruga Elbasanit 85.
Tel: (04) 237 3407.
www.tiranahostel.com

Elysée ★★

A well-priced mid-range hotel on the corner with Rruga Elbasanit just east of the Bllok area and amid the main embassies. The Elysée has spacious rooms, helpful staff, free Wi-Fi and a good breakfast buffet, but there's no elevator.

Rruga Themistokli Gërmenji 2/173.
Tel: (04) 222 2880.
www.hotelelysee-al.com

Nobel ★★

A great-value mid-range hotel, just off Sheshi Skënderbej behind the Tirana International Hotel. Clean modern rooms, a good restaurant and everything is within walking distance.

Blvd Zogu I.
Tel: (04) 225 6444.
www.hotelnobeltirana.com

Grand ★★★

The top choice in the Bllok area for many years, the Grand is a small upmarket hotel with great business facilities and a small indoor swimming pool. A mere crawl from the best addresses in town.
Rruga Ismail Qemali 11.
Tel: (04) 224 7996.
www.grandhoteltirana.com

Green House ★★★

One of the first classy boutique-style business hotels in the country, with some very sleek rooms set in a villa that also has a popular upmarket restaurant and café. Small, quiet and well appointed.
Rruga Jul Varibova 6.
Tel: (04) 222 2632.
www.greenhouse.al

Xheko Imperial ★★★

A fantastically glam hotel with outrageously kitsch suites and a rooftop restaurant straight from Hollywood. The location is great, in a quiet part of the Bllok area.
Rruga Dëshmorët e 4 Shkurtit.
Tel: (04) 225 9575.
www.xheko-imperial.com

Rogner Europapark ★★★★

The most pleasant upmarket hotel in town, with top-notch services, decent-sized rooms that are well equipped for business, and a lovely tropical garden and swimming pool at the back. The lobby area also holds the Avis car rental agency and several other useful services.
Blvd Dëshmorët e Kombit.
Tel: (04) 223 5035.
www.hotel-europapark.com

Sheraton ★★★★

An international player with all the modern facilities you would expect of the chain. In the complex there's a mall with restaurants, cafés and a cinema. Rooms at the back of the building have views of the Grand Park. Avis has an office here as well, and there's a good travel agent.
Sheshi Italia.
Tel: (04) 227 4707.
www.sheraton.com

EATING OUT

Ashiana ★★

The only Indian restaurant in Albania, it serves a variety of north and south Indian curries and other specialities, prepared by Indian cooks with imported spices. It's as authentic as it gets. For a good-value lunch, ask for the *thali* dish.
Rruga Dervish Hima.
Tel: 069 277 4459.
Open: 11am–11pm.

Juvenilja Castelo ★★

This is one of several restaurants spread around the park, but the dining halls and large terrace mean that this castle-like building is usually packed with happy diners. It serves Albanian and Italian food – you can't go wrong. Beyond the Sheraton on the edge of the Grand Park forest.
Rruga Gjeneral Niko Pushkini.
Tel: (04) 226 6666.
Open: 10am–midnight.

Era ★★★

Very popular with foreigners and expats, this Albanian restaurant in the Bllok serves all the favourite local dishes as well as Italian specialities. If you're new to the game, ask the waiters for a recommendation.
Rruga Ismail Qemali 33.
Tel: (04) 225 7805.
Open: 10am–midnight.

Rozafa ★★★

Tirana's best fish restaurant comes in two

varieties: a cheap restaurant along the main street and a more exclusive basement restaurant around the back, which is well worth the expense. Choose from freshly caught sea and river fish, enticingly displayed on shredded ice.
Rruga Luigj Gurakuqi 2.
Tel: (04) 222 786.
www.rozafa.al.
Open: noon–midnight.

Vila Ambasador Chocolat ★★★
This impressive old villa along a quiet road in the city centre has been turned into a wonderful restaurant serving local and international dishes. Have your lunch or dinner in the stylish rooms or on the leafy terrace outside.
Rruga Asim Zeneli.
Tel: (04) 225 4844.
Open: 8am–midnight.

ENTERTAINMENT

Akademia e Filmit & Multimedias Marubi (Academy of Film and Multimedia Marubi)
Every Thursday at 7pm the cinema of the film academy has free screenings of art-house movies. Check the website to see what's on next. Closed in summer.
Rruga Aleksandër Moisiu 76. Tel: (04) 236 5188.
www.afmm.edu.al

Charl's Bistro
A very lively and popular bar with indoor and outdoor areas that are crammed with the young and beautiful sipping cocktails. Ask inside if there are any band performances planned during your visit.
Rruga Pjeter Bogdani 36.
www.charlsbistro.com.
Open: 24hrs.

Imperial
Tirana's newest cinema, inside the mall attached to the Sheraton, has good modern seats and shows Hollywood blockbusters. Tickets are cheap.
Sheshi Italia.
Tel: (04) 226 6396.
www.empire-al.com

Living Room
A restaurant, café, bar and club. Attracting a young professional crowd, there's good international food to be had before you head to the club or up onto the rooftop terrace where there's a lounge area with views over town.
Rruga Presidenti George W Bush 16.
Tel: 069 203 3224.
Open: 7pm–3am.

Lollipop
A hopping club placed conveniently opposite Charl's Bistro in the Bllok area. Playing mainly house and electro for students and other young-at-heart people, it's the best address for dancing in the centre.
Rruga Pjeter Bogdani 32.
www.myspace.com/ lollipoptirana.
Open: Sun–Thur 10pm–2am, Fri & Sat 10pm–5am.

Millennium 2
The former Pioneer Palace is now a slightly worn cinema showing big Hollywood productions.
Rruga Murat Toptani.
Tel: (04) 225 3654.
www.ida-millennium.com

Teatri i Kukullave (Puppet Theatre)
A great experience for children, Tirana's fun little Puppet Theatre puts on regular shows.
Sheshi Austria, off Sheshi Skënderbej.
Tel: (04) 222 2446.

Teatri i Operas dhe Ballet (Opera and Ballet Theatre)

Keep an eye on posters or ask at the box office about upcoming opera, ballet and other performances in the Pallatin e Kulturës (Palace of Culture).
Sheshi Skënderbej.
Tel: (04) 222 4753.

Venue

A large club in the northeastern suburbs of town (any taxi driver will know where it is) that blasts ear-deafening house at the crowd of revellers. In summer the club closes and moves its activities to the Tropikal resort on the beach of Durrës.
Rruga Sadik Petrela 20.
www.venuedanceclub.com.
Open: Fri & Sat 9pm–5am.

SPORT AND LEISURE
Outdoor Albania

Your one-stop address for adventure. OA can organise all kinds of outdoor activities, from hiking or biking day trips near Tirana to week-long trips with rafting, kayaking, mountaineering, paragliding, snow-shoe trekking and guided cultural tours. See the website or contact their office at the Tirana Backpacker Hostel for more details.
Rruga Elbasanit 85.
Tel: (04) 222 7121.
www.outdooralbania.com

Vila Park Gym

Apart from the gyms at the upmarket hotels, this is perhaps Tirana's best-equipped gym. Set beside the Vila Park Hotel inside the Grand Park.
Tel: (04) 225 6597.

CENTRAL ALBANIA
Berat

ACCOMMODATION
Mangalemi ★

Good-value accommodation inside a traditional Berat house, popular with visiting NGO officials and an excellent spot for something to eat. The rooms are basic but presentable, plus there's the added bonus of a dial-up Internet connection for 125 lekë per hour. On the left at the bottom of the hill up to the castle. The price includes breakfast, for which there's even a vegetarian option.
Tel: (032) 320 93 &
068 242 9803.

Email: hotel_mangalemi_tomi@yahoo.com

Palma ★

With several doubles and triples next to the footbridge over the river, the Palma's been completely renovated and offers top-value accommodation with the added bonus of a decent restaurant on the roof. The rooms are basic, but all are en-suite and air-conditioned and come with satellite television. The best value in town by a mile.
Tel: (032) 321 43 &
069 209 3812.

Rezidenca Desaret ★

A new, traditional-style hotel in the Mangalemi area with fantastic views over the town from the large balconied rooms and a large garden with a terrace. Excellent value for money. Reach it by following the steep alley up opposite the Mangalemi Hotel.
Lagja 13 Shtatori.
Tel: (032) 375 93.

EATING OUT
Ajka ★

Across the river from the action and worth

walking over the footbridge for the view it affords, this popular venue that calls itself a taverna churns out classic Albania roast meat dishes and plenty of alcohol. There is a choice of indoor or outdoor seating, and large tables make it a good place for groups.
Tel: (032) 340 34.
Open: 8am–midnight.

Palma ★

On top of the hotel of the same name, student waiters in bow ties ferry plates of grilled meat to a wide range of diners including locals with money, foreign NGO workers and a handful of tourists. Notable for the view, Palma turns into a club later in the evening. Don't try having a romantic candlelit dinner here after 10pm on a Friday.
Tel: (032) 321 43.

Onufri ★

Inside the citadel, there's even an English menu in this tiny local-speciality restaurant, but be warned that it doesn't include the best dishes. All the authentic food,

including things such as fresh venison, need to be asked for. A good range of drinks is available, and the place does occasionally turn into a bit of a party.
Open: 10am–10pm.

Mangalemi ★★

Inside the hotel of the same name, Mangalemi provides a wide range of both local and international dishes and is also a great spot for breakfast. As well as a pleasantly recreated Albanian home setting, the restaurant also has a large open terrace with fabulous views of the town below and the castle on the hill.
Tel: (032) 320 93 & 068 242 9803.

ENTERTAINMENT

Palma

Berat's hippest location can be found on the roof of the hotel of the same name. As well as providing a menu of local and international dishes, Palma also acts as the town's night-club. Sophisticated it isn't, but if you want a night out in Berat complete with

loud pop music and the occasional bit of dancing, this is the place you need.
Tel: (032) 344 62.
Open: Sun–Thur 10am–midnight, Fri & Sat 10am–2am.

Durrës

ACCOMMODATION

Mediterran ★

A simple family-run hotel right in the old centre of town, behind the Torre defence tower and city walls. Rooms are reasonable, with TV, air-conditioning and fridge. The owner rents out his yacht for boating trips.
Rruga Kolonel Tomson. Tel: (052) 270 74. Email: mediterran@yahoo.com

Ani ★★

A neat and modern hotel along the sea-front boulevard near the museum with decent-sized rooms and a garden with palm trees. Internet is available for guests, too.
Shëtitorja Taulantia. Tel: (052) 242 28. Email: anihoteldurres@yahoo.it

Iliria Internacional ★★

A good mid-range option along Durrës' long beach south of the city centre and beside the pier leading to the eponymous disco – which means the rooms at the back will be quieter. The airy restaurant serves good seafood dishes.

Lagja 13, Iliria beach. Tel: (052) 609 65. www. iliriainternacional.com

Adriatik ★★★

The best hotel outside of Tirana is located on Durrës beach, a few kilometres from the city centre. Each floor has its own art theme, and rooms come with all possible comforts. A pleasant palm garden faces the hotel's clean stretch of beach. With top-notch business facilities, it's popular year-round.

Lagjja 13, Plazh. Tel: (052) 608 51. www.adriatikhotel.com

EATING OUT

Fish House ★★

Fresh fish and other seafood fried, grilled or poached as you like it, and various Albanian and Italian dishes served in a friendly restaurant near the city centre.

Llagja 1, Shëtitorja Taulantia.

Tel: (052) 356 66. Open: 8am–10pm.

Picante ★★

A swanky bar and restaurant along the promenade, with great views over the sea. Serving fish and Albanian food accompanied by Italian and French wine, the chef's speciality is Florentina beefsteak.

Llagja 1, Shëtitorja Taulantia. Tel: (052) 385 86. Open: 9am–11pm.

ENTERTAINMENT

Disko Iliria

Consisting of several circular terraces perched at the end of a long pier on Durrës beach, the Iliria attracts a young crowd of partygoers dancing to house, electro and Latino music.

Plazhi Iliria. Tel: 069 205 5609. Open: 6pm–2am.

Kantina e Pijeve Skënderbeu

The tasting room of a modern winery just east of Durrës allows you to sample and buy good Albanian wine at the source.

Rruga Bajram Tusha, Rrashbull. Tel: (052) 646 28. www. kantina-skenderbeu.com

Port Side

The best bar in the centre, with terraces, lounge corners and a good basement club that regularly hosts parties with DJs from Albania and abroad in the summer season. It overlooks the city walls on one side, and the port on the other.

Sheshi Taulantia. Tel: (052) 371 29. www.portsideclub.net. Open: 7am–1am.

Torre Bar

This round defence tower has been converted into a pleasant bar, with a terrace in the adjacent park, a cool room inside and a rooftop terrace with good views over the port.

Rruga Taulantia. Open: 8am–midnight.

Tropical

A massive beach resort along Durrës beach, with swimming pools, a private beach with chair rental, restaurants and bars. Most famous for the big parties held in summer with international DJs and hundreds of young visitors.

Plepa. Tel: (052) 626 69. www.tropikal.com.al. Open: 7am–3am.

Elbasan
ACCOMMODATION
Skampa ★
The traditional Communist behemoth in the town centre is at the time of writing undergoing total renovation. The rooms are small, but then again so's the bill. Great value for a no-frills overnight stay in the heart of the town.
Tel: (054) 526 61.

EATING OUT
Real Scampis ★★
Inside the old castle, a huge affair with several terraces and a nice garden. The food is Italian but the service remains entirely Albanian. During the summer the Real Scampis' outdoor terraces also serve as the town's hot night-spot.
Tel: (054) 401 62. Open: 7am–11pm.

NORTHERN ALBANIA
Lezha
ACCOMMODATION
Liss ★
Lezha's prime hotel, set on the main street, offers very simple but clean rooms with old wooden furniture and funky 1970s tiles. There's a restaurant downstairs. A good place to break the trip between Tirana and the north – but not for a longer stay.
Sheshi Besëlidhja. Tel: (021) 524 51. Email: uldedaj@icc.al.eu.org

Sebastiano ★
A lovely place to relax for a few days, Sebastiano has a fantastic fish restaurant, a good swimming pool and two villas. Surrounded by marshland and lagoons and just 20 minutes from a quiet beach. To find it, just follow the asphalt from the Ishull-Lezha turning on the main road south of Lezha.
Ishull-Lezha. Tel: 069 216 8973 & 068 225 6406.

EATING OUT
Hotel i Gjuetisë ★★
The hotel rooms of the 1930s hunting lodge of Mussolini's son-in-law and Italy's wartime minister of foreign affairs are very run down and in bad need of investment, but the restaurant continues to serve very good seafood dishes and salads. Inside, the dining room is quite impressive. Just beyond Sebastiano at the end of the asphalt road.
Ishull-Lezha. Tel: 069 217 0898. Open: 8am–10pm.

Sebastiano ★★★
An excellent fish and game restaurant that's well worth the short detour from the main road. The top-notch food includes skewered shrimps, grilled eel (held live in a small pond) and *levrek* (sea bass). Diners can use the lovely swimming pool. For directions, see Accommodation above.
Ishull-Lezha. Tel: 069 216 8973 & 068 225 6406. Open: 7am–10pm.

Lura Lakes
ACCOMMODATION
Hotel Turismi ★
Currently the only hotel in the Lura National

Park, with simple rooms and a restaurant in a mountain cabin-style building near the lakes. A good base for hikes in the surrounding area. Bookings can be made via their Tirana travel agent.

Lura National Park. Reservations via Lura Tours. Tel: (04) 222 1711. www.luratours.com

Peshkopi
ACCOMMODATION
Korabi ★

The former state hotel on the main boulevard has one wing with upgraded but simple rooms that are usually offered to foreigners. There's a shaded terrace out front, a restaurant, and enclosed parking around the back.

Rruga Elez Isuf Ndreu. Tel: 068 207 0107 & (021) 824 81.

Shëngjin
ACCOMMODATION
Ermiri Palace ★★

This newly renovated sea-front hotel in the middle of Shëngjin has good, modern rooms with sea views, a café and a very nice terrace

restaurant serving fresh seafood and other Albanian dishes.

Shëngjin beachfront. Tel: (028) 124 44. www.ermiripalace.com

Shkodra
ACCOMMODATION
Marku ★

On the hillside just across the bridge over the Buna, Marku is a large complex with a restaurant, an impressive scale model of the castle and two hotel buildings with great views of Lake Shkodra. A short taxi ride from the city centre.

Shkodra–Shiroka road. Tel: (022) 417 71.

Colosseo ★★

A decent business hotel right opposite the main mosque in the centre of town. Recently expanded, it has good facilities and a nice restaurant terrace.

Rruga 13 Dhjetori/Kolë Idromeno. Tel: (022) 475 13. www.colosseohotel.com

Europa Grand Hotel ★★

Shkodra's top hotel is a towering mirror-glass building beside the park in the city centre. Rooms are of international

standard and have windows that open so you're not dependent on the air-conditioning. There's a rooftop bar and a small pool in the hotel garden.

Sheshi 2 Prilli. Tel: (022) 412 11. www. europagrandhotel.com

EATING OUT
Perla ★

A new wooden restaurant halfway between Shkodra and the Koman ferry with tables set romantically along the lakeside on a manicured lawn. The kitchen serves international cuisine including fish and is run by an Albanian who spent years in England working with Italian chefs; the pasta dishes are exceptional as a result. There are two guest rooms upstairs, too.

Vau i Dejës lakeside, Koman road. Tel: 069 354 3605. Open: 11am–9.30pm.

Çoçja ★★

Excellent Italian and Albanian cuisine served in a beautifully renovated villa beside the Orthodox

church. With a bar and garden on the ground floor, the restaurant is upstairs with a very pleasant shaded terrace. Some Albanian specialities that are otherwise rarely found in restaurants are available, but only if you order a day in advance.
Rruga Vaso Kadia/ Hasan Riza Pasha. Tel: (022) 407 99. Open: 8am–midnight.

Taverna Shkodrana ★★
Along the shore of Lake Shkodra between Shiroka and Zogaj, the rustic Taverna Shkodrana is famous not only for the fresh lake fish and seafood served by the affable owner, but also for its excellent traditional live music sessions on Sunday afternoons.
Shiroka–Zogaj road. Tel: 069 225 9646. Open: 11am–11pm.

Tradita G&T ★★
Set in an atmospheric stone building in the city centre, Tradita is the best place to go for traditional Albanian food. There's grilled lamb from the large fireplace, or try the delicious grilled feta

cheese starter. The English-speaking owner has a fantastic collection of traditional Albanian costumes, with some very impressive bell-shaped *xhubleta* dresses from the northern mountains; ask him for a tour.
Rruga Skënderbej/ Edit Durham. Tel: 068 208 6056. Open: 7am–1am.

ENTERTAINMENT
Cuba Bar
A fun Cuban-themed bar near the university decorated with the obligatory painting of Che as well as a map and some sombreros. Very lively at night. If it's full, there are several loud and popular bars in the building next door.
Rruga Vaso Kadia/ Hasan Riza Pasha. Open: 7am–10pm.

Thethi
ACCOMMODATION
Nika Guesthouse ★
At the southern end of the village, near the path to the rapids and waterfall, this family guesthouse has ten beds available in three rooms.

Thethi Ndërlysa. Tel: 069 334 6423.

Rupa Guesthouse ★
An old farmhouse with several simple guest rooms and modern bathrooms set in the centre of Thethi, near the church and *kulla* tower. English is spoken by the younger family members.
Thethi centre. Tel: (022) 451 45. Email: rorupaog@yahoo.com

Valbona
ACCOMMODATION
Relindja and Valley Guesthouse ★
Basic but good accommodation in one of four rooms above the bar in the wooden Relindja cabin, or in the bunk-bedded rooms of the old family house in the quaint hamlet just beyond. The price includes three meals per day. Camping is possible here, too. Alfred, the English-speaking owner, is best contacted by sending an SMS message to his mobile number (*see below*), as phone reception is dodgy.
Valbona. Tel: 069 217 3603.

Vermoshi

ACCOMMODATION

Rizaj Guesthouse ★

One room sleeping four people in a small, pretty farmhouse near the centre of Vermoshi village. A great place to experience real Albanian village life, with all manner of animals scampering around. Farmer Nikolin, who also runs the village bar, has a Montenegrin mobile number (*see below*); have an Albanian speaker call or SMS.
Vermoshi.
Tel: (+ 382 69) 460 712.

SOUTHEASTERN ALBANIA

Dardha

ACCOMMODATION

Private rooms can be found in various village houses. It's best to ask around to see what's available.

Shtëpia e Pushimit Dardhë ★

The old state holiday hotel is privatised but still has rather basic rooms with shared facilities, all at dirt-cheap prices. Newer rooms have bunk beds. There's a restaurant with pool table downstairs.
Dardha centre.
Tel: 069 266 6010.

Korça

ACCOMMODATION

Grand ★

Close to where the buses arrive from Greece, the rooms come in two standards, the more expensive ones giving you a little more space and new beds but not much else. Still very much Communist in look and feel, the hotel offers a breakfast that's worth missing to have an extra hour in bed. A local man keeps an eye on your car when he's not watching television.
Main square.
Tel: (082) 431 68.

Han Elbasan ★

One of the very few traditional *hans* (inns) in the Balkans that still functions as a hotel, albeit a very, very basic one. A handful of rooms above the main gate have been upgraded for foreigners, who also get to use the clean shared bathroom. Cheap as chips and unforgettable.
Rruga Naum Kristo Vokopoja.
Tel: (082) 466 25.

Smerald ★

A small and colourfully painted hotel in a quiet location just off the northern end of Blvd Republika. It has modern facilities, friendly staff and a bright café-restaurant. Near to the park and a short walk from the city centre.
Rruga Viktimat e Pojanit 1. Tel: (082) 450 93.
Email: hotelsmerald@ yahoo.com

Regency ★★

A hotel in a quiet location behind the Grand, owned by Albanian Americans and of a decent standard. All rooms have air-conditioning, double glazing and proper heating in winter.
Rruga Ismail Qemali 7.
Tel: (082) 438 68.
www.regencyalbania.com

EATING OUT

Taverna Qilari ★★

This charming but chilly basement restaurant decorated with all manner of quirky objects serves some of the best food in town. A good place to taste the local *kernace* (sausages) or *qofta Korça* (meatballs in tomato sauce). Turn right two streets north of the Kinema Majestik.

Rruga Bardhyl Pojani 8.
Tel: 069 248 9693.
Open: 1pm–11pm.

Taverna Vasili ★★

The most elegant Albanian restaurant in town, with two floors of seating and excellent traditional food. Near the northern end of Blvd Republika, and around the corner from the Smerald hotel.

Rruga Kostadina Gaçe.
Tel: (082) 466 10.
Open: noon–11pm.

ENTERTAINMENT

Moska Bar

A very swanky bar on the first and second floor of a building along the main road, with a pleasant rooftop terrace. There are Russian paintings and an extravagant wine room to admire. Serves various international beers and local brands.

Blvd Republika.
Tel: 069 225 5999.
Open: 7am–midnight.

Përmet

ACCOMMODATION

Përmeti ★

In the main square you'll find this good-value hotel with a range of both dingy and renovated rooms, all excellent value for money. The en-suite facilities have showers only, and there's not much else extra in the rooms. Try to get a room at the front of the building, as they all come with splendid views of the square.

Tel: 068 208 6977.

EATING OUT

Stiliani ★

A cute little pizza joint on two floors around the back of the main square. Also on offer are grilled meat and kebabs.

Sheshi i Hotelit.
Tel: 069 287 8040.
Open: 9am–midnight.

Pogradec

ACCOMMODATION

Royal ★

Completely renovated on the edge of the lake, the rooms are immaculate and the views are stunning, although the

ones facing the sunrise don't have curtains. Breakfast is served on the roof.

Rruga Reshit Çollaku.
Tel: (083) 231 58.
Fax: (083) 231 59.

Vila Bimbli ★★

A modern and basic hotel complete with a decent bar and restaurant, next to Parku i Qytetit and overlooking the lake. All rooms come with en-suite facilities and little else. The best location in town.

Tel: (083) 225 16 &
069 223 2057.

EATING OUT

Tea ★

An Albanian-only menu offers pizza, fish and the usual grilled meat dishes, brought to your table by chain-smoking waiters. Tea also has accommodation upstairs and does a brave job at doubling as the local bar. The depressingly early closing time is often ignored, and the small terrace provides a decent spot for an evening drink or two.

Tel: (083) 229 47.
Open: 7am–10pm.

Voskopoja
ACCOMMODATION
Akademia ★
This rather grand-looking collection of buildings around a well-tended garden in the hills just north of Voskopoja has neat, simple rooms with heating and TV. The ballroom-sized dining room in the restaurant building recalls the original holiday camp origins of the complex.
Voskopoja.
Tel: 069 225 8646.

EATING OUT
Ura e Kovacë ★★
One of two trout farms and restaurants along the road up to Voskopoja, with a pet bear called Bruno in an enclosure. There's pleasant seating between the gurgling canals of the trout ponds, and the fish is as fresh as it can be.
Korça–Velipoja road.
Tel: 069 209 4109.
Open: 10am–10pm.

SOUTHERN ALBANIA
The best nightlife on the Albanian Riviera can be found dotted along the region's many beaches. Most are little more than temporary bars set up near the water and are open only for the short season from around the start of July until mid-September.

Butrint
ACCOMMODATION
Livia ★★
Twelve very nice rooms complete with air-conditioning and limited satellite television, right next to the archaeological site and overlooking the Ionian Sea. All rooms are en-suite, plus there's a decent restaurant and garden at the front. Prices are for the room, not per person.
Tel: 069 205 1263.

EATING OUT
Livia ★★★
White tablecloths, air-conditioning and something approaching silver service, plus a menu that includes stuffed vine leaves, octopus salad, mussels, squid, pork, veal and chicken. Also a small dessert menu and a few well-chosen local and international wines.
Tel: 069 205 1263.
Open: 24hrs.

Dhërmi
ACCOMMODATION
Dorian ★★★
Sitting on a hairpin bend in a forest, this rather plain hotel has a few rooms that can fit from four to six people, complete with en-suite bathrooms and little else. The water comes from the mountain, and there's a small restaurant. The hotel charges per room – sharing will drop the cost considerably.
Tel: 068 244 8049.

Gjirokastra
ACCOMMODATION
Kalemi ★
Tucked away up behind the Ethnographic Museum close to the centre of the old town, Kalemi offers a choice of basic rooms decorated in the traditional Gjirokastra style complete with fabulous carved ceilings. Breakfast and great views of the

town included. Note that Kalemi is hugely popular with foreigners, and as it has only ten rooms, booking in advance is highly recommended. English is spoken via email although not necessarily in the guesthouse itself.
Tel: (084) 637 24 & 068 223 4373. Email: draguak@yahoo.com

Sopoti ★

Inside a fabulous 100-year-old building at the top of the square, this place provides the bare basics, namely a room with a bed and little else plus shared bathroom facilities. For the price you'd be mad to complain, plus the rooms at the front have wonderful balconies with views of the castle. The best budget option in town. If there's nobody in reception, nip into the bar next door and ask for Shemedim.
Tel: (084) 264 4220.

Venus ★

Basic and modern twins and doubles with en-suite facilities, air-conditioning and balconies. Situated next to the main minibus stop

in the new part of town, so it's a long walk from the main sights but useful if you're arriving with a lot of luggage and can't be bothered to move any further. There's an attached bar on the ground floor.
Junction of Blvd 18 Shtatori & Rruga Nacionale.
Tel: (084) 688 40.

EATING OUT
Festivali ★

Not as posh as Fantazia (*see below*) but the better of the two for atmosphere and the classic local experience. The town's former Moscow Restaurant is decorated with some nice wooden folk motifs and has an extraordinary mosaic of seven men in local costumes dancing, the work of D Cuberi and J Mici and dating from 1981. The menu features everything from frogs' legs to *qifqi*, a Gjirokastra speciality of seasoned, fried rice balls cooked in a special pan for the purpose, all of it served with huge salads and big chunks of

wonderful fried bread. Recommended.
Open: 8am–10pm.

ENTERTAINMENT
Fantazia

The nightlife in the new part of town is not at all recommended. Your best bet is to enjoy the outdoor terrace of Fantazia, where locals come to drink and talk into the night. Like most night-spots outside the capital, this place also doubles as a restaurant, making it a great location to eat first before finding a spot on the terrace (where a huge statue of Enver Hoxha once stood) and making friends with the locals. Note that Fantazia opens at 6am for coffee. Food starts four hours later.
Tel: (084) 680 55.
Open: Sun–Thur 10am–midnight, Fri & Sat 10am–2am.

Himara
ACCOMMODATION
Gjoka ★

A threadbare classic next to the bus station, this waterfront hotel is ideal for young independent travellers on a shoe-

string budget. The facilities are old and basic, to say the least.
Tel: 069 207 6016.

Rapo's Resort ★★
A brand new holiday hotel with a great pool and its own private beach. The whole place looks like it's been furnished from Ikea, but the staff are more than friendly. Just south of the town centre on the road to Saranda. Top marks, however, for a website that actually works.
Tel: (039) 328 56.
www.raposresorthotel.com

EATING OUT
Magjia e Chimerës ★★★★
Wine glasses on the tables and a huge grandfather clock mark Magjia e Chimerës as, visually at least, a cut above the rest. Handy for breakfast and complete with a small terrace right on the edge of the water, it offers mains including pasta, meat and horrendously expensive seafood. The fish may be great but the service may leave you feeling you've not quite got value for

money. Find it next to the bus station in the centre of town.
Tel: (039) 322 63.
Open: 6am–midnight.

Ksamil
ACCOMMODATION
Sejko ★
A modern round building close to the shore and near the islands, its rooms are basic, to say the least. Some come with en-suite facilities. Handy for the beach but hardly a luxury option. Excellent views if you get a room at the front of the building.
Tel: 069 313 1311.

Arturi ★★
If you're looking for a modern hotel with everything you need but no extra frills and with its own private beach, Arturi will make you very happy indeed. Just north of the town proper, this makes an excellent base for exploring the area south of Saranda, with a decent in-house seafood restaurant to boot (*see below*).
Tel: 069 254 3932.

EATING OUT
Arturi ★
This new and rather clinical venture in the hotel of the same name (*see above*) specialises in cheap, quality seafood dishes including squid, mussels, eel and cuttlefish. The view from the terrace is truly wonderful.
Tel: 069 254 3932.
Open: 6am–2am.

Llogora Pass
ACCOMMODATION
Fshati Turistik ★★
Smack bang on top of the pass and signposted off the western side of the main Saranda–Vlora road, the 'Tourist Village' is well worth having a look at if not sleeping in. A series of well-appointed wooden chalets all with two bedrooms plus living room, satellite television and minibar are laid out in a shady green area. The park comes with its own wild deer, an excellent restaurant and facilities for children. Tours around the area are also possible.
Tel: 068 212 8640.

Saranda

ACCOMMODATION

Hairy Lemon Hostel ★

A welcome addition to Saranda's large, albeit uniform, accommodation options, this fairly new venture provides the classic hostel experience. The facilities are basic but clean and new, and the location, just north of the ferry terminal and a ten-minute walk from the centre, is perfect for people arriving from Corfu or those who want to stay away from the noise and chaos that the summer evenings often bring to the town.
Tel: 069 355 9317.

Kaonia ★★

On the waterfront very close to the harbour, this is a good choice if you don't mind fumbling your way to your room in the dark and suffering a constant lack of Internet facilities – which you pay for as part of the deal. The rooms, however, are fine, many of them with wonderful balconies overlooking the sea. Great location, too.
Lagija 2.

Tel: (085) 226 00. Email: kaoniahotel@yahoo.com

Palma ★★

A Norwegian-run hotel next to the ferry terminal with a limited choice of rooms and suites, all coming with air-conditioning, satellite television and en-suite bathrooms. Discounts on group bookings. Ten minutes from the centre.
Tel: (085) 229 29.

Syri i Kalter ★★

Five very basic chalets in a secluded forest clearing. Toilet facilities are shared. The price is 5,000 lekë per chalet all year round, and each chalet sleeps up to four people.
Syri i Kalter springs.
Tel: 069 403 8201.

Butrinti ★★★

Conference rooms, a swimming pool, Wi-Fi Internet, a decent bar and business-class rooms all work together to create the effect of a classy hotel. However, service lets the side down. A good location at the southern end of the promenade, but a little expensive for what it really is.
Tel: (085) 255 92. Email: hotelbutrint@hotmail.com

EATING OUT

La Bananna ★

Omelettes, coffee, toast and marmalade for breakfast in a basic courtyard full of banana plants. Later in the day the menu includes more ambitious dishes such as pasta salad and the usual array of grilled meat and fresh fish landed on the quay just over a stone's throw away.
Shetitorja e Qytetit.
Tel: (085) 243 63.
Open: 7am–11pm.

Syri i Kalter ★

Good old-fashioned barbecue-style cooking featuring plenty of roast meat and salad, all in the hotel of the same name (*see above*). There's a fireplace for those brave enough to visit in the winter, plus a lovely terrace on the edge of a running stream.
Tel: 069 403 8201.
Open: 6am–midnight.

Limani ★★

On the harbour halfway along the esplanade, this decent pizza restaurant serves 16 better-than-average meat, fish and vegetarian pizzas plus one 'chilly' pizza, delivered to

tables both inside and out by a handful of friendly waiters. A magnificent location, and drinks include Tirana beer and a fine freshly squeezed red orange juice.
Tel: (085) 258 58.
Open: 6am–midnight.

ENTERTAINMENT
Mango
Two kilometres (1¼ miles) south of the centre by the Cuka Channel, this rather classy beach complex has by far the most exciting bar and club in the area. The best of the country's DJs play here, and the nights can be long and loud. Excellent fun indeed.
Tel: 068 209 9166. Open: bar and club Sun–Thur 6pm–midnight, Fri & Sat 6pm–4am. Closed: winter.

Vlora
ACCOMMODATION
Paradise Beach ★★★
Just south of the little tunnel on the road heading towards Saranda, Paradise Beach offers a decent base away from the city centre complete with its own private beach. The rooms are straight out of

a showroom, all coming with air-conditioning, satellite television and room service. There's a huge restaurant as well.
Tel: 069 209 5154.

Vlora International ★★★
Handy for the international ferry and a short walk from the main sights, this relatively expensive hotel remains more than affordable for most Western travellers (what you pay here is less than a night in basic bed and breakfast in the UK). The overall service falls into the *Fawlty Towers* category, but the little extras, including free LAN and wireless internet in every room, a sparkling swimming pool and a bar with spectacular views, more than make up for its shortcomings.
Tel: (033) 244 08. www. vlorainternational.com

EATING OUT
Kristal ★
Next to the Independence Museum and the port, this might possibly be the only fast-food restaurant in the world that makes its own French fries. Excellent if you can't wait

to eat, alongside the menu of dishes made to order in the kitchen is a range of ready-to-eat meals.
Tel: 069 281 4006.
Open: 7am–11pm.

ENTERTAINMENT
The entire beach from end to end is covered with bars and small clubs pumping out loud music throughout the night during the height of the summer season.

Alternatively, try:
Vlora International
The bar on the first floor of the port-side hotel fills during the summer evenings with locals and tourists looking for a little bit of sophistication. The bar is one of the best stocked in the city, and there are even complimentary snacks with drinks. Choose the air-conditioned indoor space complete with MTV, or the view of the port from the large rooftop terrace.
Tel: (033) 244 08.
Open: Sun–Thur 6pm–midnight, Fri & Sat 6pm–2am.

158

Index

Acknowledgements

Thomas Cook wishes to thank the photographers for the loan of the photographs reproduced in this book, to whom copyright in the photographs belongs.

JEROEN VAN MARLE 1, 4, 9, 12, 15, 18, 20, 21, 25, 30, 31, 32, 33, 36, 38, 39, 41, 43, 45, 53, 57, 58, 59, 60, 62, 63, 64, 67, 70, 71, 73, 76, 77, 78, 79, 109, 110, 111, 113, 115, 117, 123, 124, 125, 126, 127, 133, 134, 136
RICHARD SCHOFIELD 5, 6, 13, 14, 24, 26, 27, 44, 49, 50, 51, 54, 55, 75, 80, 82, 83, 85, 86, 87, 88, 89, 90, 91, 92, 93, 95, 96, 97, 98, 99, 100, 101, 104, 105, 106, 107, 119, 121, 131
MJAFT! ALBANIA 19
GTZ SHKODRA 66, 69, 72
GAZMEND KERKUTI 108
OUTDOOR ALBANIA 129, 140

For CAMBRIDGE PUBLISHING MANAGEMENT LTD:
Project editor: Karen Beaulah
Typesetter: Paul Queripel
Copy editor: Anne McGregor
Proofreader: Karolin Thomas
Indexer: Karolin Thomas

SEND YOUR THOUGHTS TO
BOOKS@THOMASCOOK.COM

We're committed to providing the very best up-to-date information in our travel guides and constantly strive to make them as useful as they can be. You can help us to improve future editions by letting us have your feedback. If you've made a wonderful discovery on your travels that we don't already feature, if you'd like to inform us about recent changes to anything that we do include, or if you simply want to let us know your thoughts about this guidebook and how we can make it even better – we'd love to hear from you.

Send us ideas, discoveries and recommendations today and then look out for your valuable input in the next edition of this title.

Emails to the above address, or letters to Travellers Series Editor, Thomas Cook Publishing, PO Box 227, Coningsby Road, Peterborough PE3 8SB, UK.

Please don't forget to let us know which title your feedback refers to!